Reflective Teaching in Primary Schools

Transforming Primary QTS

Reflective Learning and Teaching in Primary Schools

Edited by Alice Hansen

Los Angeles | London | New Delhi
Singapore | Washington DC

Learning Matters
An imprint of SAGE Publications Ltd
1 Oliver's Yard
55 City Road
London EC1Y 1SP

SAGE Publications Inc.
2455 Teller Road
Thousand Oaks, California 91320

SAGE Publications India Pvt Ltd
B1/I 1 Mohan Cooperative Industrial Area
Mathura Road
New Delhi 110 044

SAGE Asia-Pacific Pte Ltd
3 Church Street
#10-04 Samsung Hub
Singapore 049483

Editor: Amy Thornton
Development Editor: Jennifer Clark
Production Controller: Chris Marke
Project Management: Deer Park Productions, Tavistock
Marketing Manager: Catherine Slinn
Cover Design: Toucan
Typeset by: PDQ Typesetting Ltd
Printed by: MPG Books Group, Bodmin, Cornwall

Library of Congress Control Number: 2012933565

British Library Cataloguing in Publication data

A catalogue record for this book is available from the
British Library

ISBN 978 0 85725 769 7 paperback
ISBN 978 0 85725 865 6 hardback

FSC

Contents

Acknowledgements

Lisa Murtagh wishes to offer her special thanks to trainee teachers at Edge Hill University, and in particular to Louise Barnett and Samantha Goodyear.

Contributors

Alice Hansen is the Director of Children Count Ltd where she is an educational consultant. Her work includes running professional development courses and events for teachers and teacher trainers, research and publishing. Alice has worked in education in England and abroad. Prior to her current work she was a primary mathematics tutor and the programme leader for a full-time primary PGCE programme at the University of Cumbria.

Nick Clough is currently working as a consultant for teacher and care provider education, specialising in the development of reflective practices that make improvements possible. He draws on the findings of his own doctoral work, 'Community Praxis in Rural Zimbabwe', during which he relearned the value of reflection-in-action while alongside community members who had initiated and built their own community library as a base for their cultural and educational development. Until recently he worked as a Director of Initial Teacher Education at the University of the West of England, Bristol.

Adrian Copping worked for a number of years as a primary teacher in two Lancashire primary schools before joining St Martin's College (now University of Cumbria) in 2003. Adrian leads the Lancaster campus side of the Primary PGCE, including an M-level module on Reflective Practice which he has recently written and for which he received an Excellence in Teaching and Learning award from the University. Adrian also teaches primary English and music. He is currently engaged in research into the integration of work-based and centre-based learning through co-teaching. Adrian regularly volunteers in primary schools, teaching creative thinking through English and drama and specialising in the use of teacher-in-role.

Helen Davenport worked for ten years in the Early Years sector of Birmingham, including roles as Foundation Stage Leader and Deputy Head, until joining Manchester Metropolitan University in 2008. Her major responsibility is as Year 2 Cohort Leader for the BA Primary programme, within which she also teaches on a number of Early Years units, including the Learning Through Play specialism. Helen is currently engaged in research that explores the nature of students' reflective writing, and pedagogic strategies that might embed the process of reflective journal writing more deeply and effectively. Her wider academic interests relate to play and risk-taking among children, including the pedagogies and practices stemming from Forest Schools, both in Britain and internationally.

Pete Dudley taught for many years in east London and abroad and has spent 20 years in school improvement and raising standards. For five years he was Director of the Primary National Strategy. In 2001 he began research into teacher learning through Lesson Study, a Japanese approach to improving teacher and pupil learning. He has introduced Lesson Study to the UK working with National College of School Leadership, the National Strategies, the General Teaching Council of Northern Ireland and a range of universities, local authorities and schools. Completing his doctorate at Cambridge in 2011, he now writes and speaks on Lesson Study internationally and runs www.lessonstudy.co.uk.

Elizabeth Gowing worked in primary classrooms and school leadership teams in inner London before joining a Lambeth Education Action Zone as professional development consultant. She went on to be a policy link advisor with the General Teaching Council, focusing on professional learning, and then became an independent education consultant working with local authorities, professional associations and the Primary National Strategy. Since 2006 she has divided her time between the UK and Kosovo where she is co-founder of the educational charity The Ideas Partnership, and has worked on professional development approaches with the European Union, Save the Children, Unicef and other international Non-Governmental Organisations.

Emma McVittie began her RE career as a primary school teacher where her roles included RE co-ordinator and special educational needs co-ordinator. In 2004 Emma became a Senior Lecturer in Primary RE at the University of Cumbria where she spent seven years, during which time she was the specialist course leader for both undergraduate and postgraduate teacher training courses. Emma is now an independent RE consultant and the Primary Leader for REonline as well as a regular contributor to the *REMatters* online journal. Her research interests include developing reflective practice in the primary school, whole school spiritual development, the use of creative assessment, and engaging children with spiritual literacy through neuro-linguistic programming.

Lisa Murtagh has been involved in ITT for the past 12 years. Her current role at Edge Hill University is Programme Leader for the BA (Honours) Primary Education with QTS Part-Time Programme and she is also appointed as a Research Fellow of the Centre for Learner Identity Studies. Her research interests lie in formative assessment, in the field of Primary Education and in Higher Education. The focus of Lisa's current work is aimed at enhancing assessment experiences for students already engaged in HE study, and preparing prospective students to embark upon their HE experiences with a clearer expectation of what will happen and, indeed, what they may experience, in order to allow for a more informed and smoother transition.

Mike Pezet is a professional coach who holds an MSc in Personal and Organisational Development. His research into the relationship between blame, feedback and the acceptance of feedback has been published as a practical workbook to help managers enhance their feedback skills. Mike has helped hundreds of teachers across the UK in the use of coaching skills to aid reflective practice. As a coach Mike feels privileged to be asked to help people unlock and develop their capacity to lead. He has worked with many different industries, roles and nationalities, from education, to mental health, to construction, to defence, to name a few. Coaching, for Mike, is a stimulating, continual process of learning from, and with, those he works with.

Introduction
Alice Hansen

This book has been published to help you to develop the tools and strategies you need to improve your own teaching and learning and the learning and development of the children in your care. It is full of practical advice for how to use reflection during your initial teacher training course to its fullest effect.

This extended introduction sets the scene for the book and introduces the chapters that follow. It identifies the central place reflection has in learning and teaching for children and adults, and learning to be a teacher. First, before exploring the notion of reflective learning and teaching, it is prudent to clarify how learning and teaching is defined and used within this book.

'Teaching/learning'

As a trainee teacher, when do you see yourself as a teacher and as a learner? When you are in a seminar, are you passively learning from your tutor or are you expected to discuss and support peers to learn also? When you are in the classroom, what are your expectations about the children acting as teachers to each other, that is, learning from each other? I ask these questions to challenge your thinking about the artificial divide that the terms *teaching* and *learning* in the English language can create.

To my mind you will always sit somewhere along the teaching/learning continuum illustrated in Figure I.1. Sometimes you might find yourself at one end. For example where would you place yourself now, reading this book? I imagine towards the learning end (Point A). Often, however, your placement on the continuum will be dynamic, depending on what you are doing, who you are doing it with, and how you perceive it to be going. Can you think of situations where you may be at Points A, B or C on the continuum?

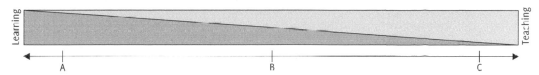

Figure I.1: The teaching/learning continuum

When you are a trainee teacher and teacher (and no doubt in many other roles in your life) you will be learning and teaching to some extent at any given time. Schön's notion of *professional artistry* (1983, pp.48–9), which will be revisited later in this introduction, reflects this. When you teach, you are consistently reflecting on your actions and those of the children in your care. Schön refers to this as *reflection in action* and this activity could be placed somewhere around Point B on the continuum. Schön also refers to *reflection on reflection in action*, where a teacher deliberately takes time to further develop his/her *repertoire of knowledge and experience* through a *conversation with the situation* (Schön, 1983, p.166). In these situations, placement is more likely to be around Point A on the continuum.

Therefore, it is rather difficult – and I suggest unnecessary – to artificially separate the two terms learning and teaching. Indeed, I hope that by the time you have read this introduction you will see that the act of 'teaching/learning' is symbiotic, that one does not exist without the other, and that reflection is a component within their relationship.

The idea of 'teaching/learning' is not a new one. For example, John-Steiner and Mahn (2003, p.133) use the term 'teaching/learning' to represent 'a joint endeavour that encompasses learners, teachers, peers, and the use of socially-constructed artefacts'. They cite Sutton (1980) as defining teaching/learning from the work of Vygotsky: 'The Russian word *obuchenie* does not admit to a direct English translation. It means both teaching and learning, both sides of the two-way process, and is therefore well suited to a dialectical view of a phenomenon made up of mutually interpenetrating opposites.'

Another term for teaching and learning is *pedagogy*. Through their ten principles for effective pedagogy, the Teaching and Learning Research Programme (TLRP) identifies evidence-informed pedagogic principles for all learner age groups and sectors in education. The principles are listed below, but you should visit the website (www.tlrp.org/themes/themes/tenprinciples.html) to read about each of them. As you work through this book, you will be able to see how you can use the principles in your own reflective practice as a learner and as a teacher to support children's development.

1. *Effective pedagogy equips learners for life in its broadest sense.*

2. *Effective pedagogy engages with valued forms of knowledge.*

3. *Effective pedagogy recognises the importance of prior experience and learning.*

4. *Effective pedagogy requires learning to be scaffolded.*

5. *Effective pedagogy needs assessment to be congruent with learning.*

6. *Effective pedagogy promotes the active engagement of the learner.*

7. *Effective pedagogy fosters both individual and social processes and outcomes.*

8. *Effective pedagogy recognises the significance of informal learning.*

9. *Effective pedagogy depends on the learning of all those who support the learning of others.*

10. *Effective pedagogy demands consistent policy frameworks with support for learning as their primary focus.*

(TLRP, online)

The chapters in this book often use learning and teaching interchangeably. When you are reading a discussion about what you can do as a learner, challenge yourself to think about how the ideas could be translated into the classroom and be used with children. Likewise, when you are reading about encouraging children to be reflective learners, step back and think about how you might use similar ideas in your own learning.

What is reflection?

Reflection is a broad concept used as a tool for learning in many different disciplines and it is a difficult notion to pin down. Biggs points out that 'a reflection in a mirror is an exact replica of what is in front of it. Reflection in professional practice, however, gives back not what it is, but what might be, an improvement on the original' (1999, p.6). Many identify reflection as a tool for 'deep' learning (Moon, 2001; Hinett, 2002; Race, 2004). Race (2004, p224) encapsulates many authors' definitions in how he talks about the impact of reflection.

> *Reflection deepens learning. The act of reflecting is one which causes us to make sense of what we've learned, why we learned it, and how that particular increment of learning took place. Moreover, reflection is about linking one increment of learning to the wider perspective of learning – heading towards seeing the bigger picture. Reflection is equally useful when our learning has been unsuccessful – in such cases indeed reflection can often give us insights into what may have gone wrong with our learning, and how on a future occasion we might avoid now-known pitfalls. Most of all, however, it is increasingly recognised that reflection is an important transferable skill, and is much valued by all around us, in employment, as well as in life in general.*

> *Race (2004)*

What is reflection in 'learning/teaching'?

John Dewey

Dewey (1933) is seen by many as the father of reflection in education. In his seminal book for teachers, *How We Think: A restatement of the relation of reflective thinking to the educative process*, he explained that reflective thinking is used by people when a solution to a problem cannot be found with certainty. This is particularly helpful to you as a trainee teacher because there is never anything certain in education, teaching and learning! Dewey defined reflective thinking as 'active, persistent, and careful consideration of any belief or supposed form of knowledge in the light of the grounds that support it and the further conclusions to which it tends' (Dewey 1933, p.118).

He went on to identify five thinking states, which are outlined below (1933, pp.199–209).

1. Dewey believed that individuals (and societies) are characterised by habitual patterns. It is only when a habit is disturbed that the process of *intellection* is employed.

2. When an individual directly experiences difficulty or perplexity then this turns into a problem that could be solved. This second stage involves an individual identifying the important aspects of the context in order to solve the problem.

3. The third stage involves identifying a hypothesis and coming up with a variety of possible solutions, perhaps through brainstorming ideas.

4. Considering and weighing up the possible solutions is the fourth stage.

5. Finally, testing the hypothesis (either in reality or by imagining) eliminates those ideas that do not work and identifies a favoured solution.

Perhaps you can see action research models you have followed reflecting these ideas more formally. This idea is discussed in more detail in Chapter 2.

Developments of Dewey's work

Many have taken Dewey's work forward and you will read a little of this in the chapters in this book. For more detail, the further reading section at the end of Chapter 2 provides suggestions for books that discuss these theorists and educationalists and their work.

King and Kitchener (2002) are researchers who used Dewey's notion of reflective thinking in their Reflective Judgement Model to define *reflective reasoning*. Their model describes how critical or reflective thinking skills are developed by adolescents moving into adulthood. The final stages of the model refer to reflective reasoning. They explain how people who use reflective reasoning accept

> *that knowledge claims cannot be made with certainty, but [they] are not immobilized by it; rather, [they] make judgments that are 'most reasonable' and about which they are 'relatively certain,' based on their evaluation of available data. They believe they must actively construct their decisions, and that knowledge claims must be evaluated in relationship to the context in which they were generated to determine their validity. They also readily admit their willingness to reevaluate the adequacy of their judgments as new data or new methodologies become available.*

> (King and Kitchener, 2002, p.40)

This is the type of reasoning that you will be expected to undertake on your initial teacher training course and beyond.

Criticisms of Dewey's work

There has been some criticism of Dewey's work. For example some feel that the five thinking states can be interpreted in a linear, process-oriented way (Smith, 1999). Approaching reflection as a systematic process is sometimes required in your professional work, as later chapters discuss in detail. For example, Chapter 2 talks further about reflection in action research.

Another criticism is that Dewey's work pays limited attention to emotions. Boud, Keogh and Walker (1985) address this. They define reflection as an activity in which people 'recapture their experience, think about it, mull it over and evaluate it' (p.19). They rework Dewey's five thinking states into three (pp.26–31).

- *Returning to experience* – retelling the salient events.
- *Attending to (or connecting with) feelings* – the purpose is twofold: identifying and building on helpful feelings and dealing with obstructive ones.
- *Evaluating experience* – analysing the experience while considering one's intent, knowledge and understanding of the event. This analysis supports the integration of new knowledge into one's existing understanding.

Later chapters address emotions in more detail. See in particular Mike Pezet's chapter on using coaching as a tool for reflection and Helen Davenport's chapter on reflective journals and portfolios.

A final criticism of Dewey's work is based on the notion that 'the individual student teacher learns to reflect on a particular experience individually' (Cinnamond and Zimpher, 1990, p.58), and that learning is not something that happens individually but is socially mediated. The social nature of reflection is revisited several times throughout this book and it is to this idea that we now turn.

Vygotsky and the social nature of learning and teaching

Social constructivism is a central theory that explains how we learn and how your role as a teacher is crucial in supporting children's cognitive development.

Vygotsky, one of the most well-known social constructivists, is perhaps most cited in relation to his work on the Zone of Proximal Development (ZPD). He defines it as 'the distance between the actual development level as determined by independent problem-solving and the level of potential to development as determined through problem-solving through adult guidance or in collaboration with more capable peers' (Vygotsky, 1978, p.86). Indeed, Eraut (1996, p.15) reminds us that interaction with a teacher and/or more capable peers is not merely desirable but is an essential requirement of development.

Think about your initial teacher training course. When do you feel you learn most effectively? What role do your peers, school colleagues and course tutors have during these times? Now think about your role as a teacher. How do you plan for children to experience the best possible learning opportunities?

The notion of the ZPD was developed by Wood, Bruner and Ross (1979), who considered how teachers and peers could build (*scaffold*) and withdraw (*fade*) support as necessary to help a child bridge the ZPD. Thinking about your course, identify where support is built and then fades appropriately. For further discussion about course design and the role of academic tutors, read Chapters 2 and 3.

Wells (1999, p.136) specifically comments on the importance of talk in Vygotsky's work:

> *Vygotsky's great contribution was to recognize that an even greater effect resulted from the development of semiotic tools based on signs, of which the most powerful and versatile is speech. For not only does speech function as a tool that mediates social action, it also provides one of the chief means – in what Vygotsky (1987) called 'inner speech' – of mediating the individual mental activities of remembering, thinking and reasoning.*

And Vygotsky explains (1978, p.280):

> *external speech is not inner speech plus sound any more than inner is external speech minus sound. The transition from inner to external speech is complex and dynamic. It is the transformation of a predicative, idiomatic speech into the syntax of differentiated speech which is comprehensible to others.*

Others have also identified talk as essential for learning. For example, Hoyles (1985) identified 'cognitive talk' that allows a child to 'step aside' and reflect on an aspect. In the first chapter, Emma McVittie continues the discussion about dialogue. Eraut (1996) also acknowledges that the wider social context is important for developing learners' understanding because their 'knowledge base' is developed through the social interaction (predominantly discussion) that occurs. He proposes, however, that even though a learner's knowledge base may share similar features with others', 'it still remains personalized and that it is important for a pupil's learning as well as their sense of identity that the personal nature of their knowledge is recognized' (p.15). John-Steiner and Mahn (2003, p.146) broaden this by explaining how our knowledge and understanding 'evolve from the sustained dynamic of individuals engaged in symbolic behaviour both with other humans, present and past, and with material and nonmaterial culture captured in books, artifacts and living memory'. Indeed, there are many aspects to consider such as how the classroom is laid out to allow particular directions of travel, groupings, access to resources, and so on (Arthur, Grainger and Wray, 2006).

So, while reflection is to some extent an internal, individual process, it does not need to be undertaken independently. Indeed, it is something that occurs most effectively when you are challenged by others through discussion of some sort. Therefore all the chapters in this book expect you to engage in dialogue – be it verbally or in another form – with children, peers and tutors throughout your course as part of your reflective practice.

Classroom norms and teacher expectations

As well as undertaking your own reflection as a trainee teacher, you also need to encourage children's reflective abilities. Emma McVittie provides many practical suggestions for doing this in Chapter 1. When analysing their own research about how children learned, Kafai and Harel (1991) referred to reflection as an 'incubation phase'. Additionally, Ackermann (1991) identified a 'cognitive dance' where children necessarily 'dive in' and 'step back' from a situation to create balance and understanding.

The discussion above about the social nature of learning and teaching, and Emma McVittie's discussion in Chapter 1 about creating a reflective classroom in practice, point to learning environments where there is a buzz in the air and where the learners and their teacher are working together to a shared outcome and developed understanding. Alongside this we also need to encourage learners to incubate their ideas to create balance and understanding. So we will turn our attention here to classroom norms and your expectations. How do you encourage this buzz and opportunity for the community of learners to reflect in your own classroom?

Yackel and Cobb (1996, p.460) offer one way forward. They discuss an evolving and increasingly sophisticated process that happens over a period of time as the teacher develops their understanding of the learners' conceptual development. This approach to classroom discussion (which Yackel and Cobb refer to as 'argumentation') is imperative because it creates the backdrop for the development of ideas. As argumentation evolves, the 'taken-as-shared communication' is subtly adjusted because it continues to form the backdrop for discussion, thus bringing about conceptual development. This validates the use of a reflective (and reflexive) approach to learning and teaching.

However, Goodchild (2001) provides a warning. He identifies a significant amount of literature that uses the phrase 'blind activity' (in contrast to reflective activity) when referring to children carrying out tasks set by their teacher. He cites Carr (1996, p.94) who states that 'students need to be made aware that [learning] is more than a set of procedural steps to be blindly followed', and Christiansen and Walther (1986, p.250) who explain that 'blind activity on a task does not ensure learning as intended'.

What activities are you encouraged to undertake as a trainee teacher, and what activities do you expect the learners in your care to participate in? When you are teaching, are you encouraging argumentation as a backdrop for children to develop their ideas? Or are you planning 'blind activity' for them instead? Which do you aspire to? How can you reach your goals?

Schön, reflection and the unique nature of every classroom situation

Teaching is complex. Its complexity is due to a huge number of variables which are in constant flux, leading to situations that are unique for every trainee teacher. Because of this, it is not possible, nor desirable, for any initial teacher training course to instruct, 'when X happens you should do Y' in a given situation. (The exception may be a child protection issue that requires a very specific, legally binding response.) In my experience many trainees can find this very challenging. They desire to become good teachers but just want to know what they should do. It is only after experiencing teaching, and as they learn more about learning and teaching, that they realise this is not an approach that will help them to become the best teacher they can be.

Schön's (1983) *reflection in action* helps to address this dilemma. He describes an iterative process, in which unresolved situations are developed into resolved situations through repeatedly defining the problem. Schön argues that while teaching, the teacher makes use of *professional artistry*. This *knowing in action* is where the teacher develops *theories in use*. These theories are created *from* the specific context *for* the specific context. They may involve scientific knowledge, but it is assumed that the teacher's experience steers the process of exploring, testing and refining/redefining theories in use. Schön explains that this can be seen as a *conversation with the situation* – a continuous communication between the teacher and others involved, as well as terminating specific avenues if they do not work, due to the *backtalk* of the situation.

How to use this book

In my work with trainee teachers and teachers the most common feedback about reflection I receive is that being reflective is a lot of additional work. However, you will already own an arsenal full of reflective tools that you have previously engaged to undertake a range of incidental or intuitive reflective activity in your professional and academic work. (You can read more about intuitive reflection in Chapter 2.) That activity has helped you to develop into the person and professional you are now. This book is designed to take your reflective practice beyond where it currently sits. It will extend the theory and ideas presented to you in this chapter and help you to make more use of those tools you have as well as introduce new ones. You will notice yourself moving around the learning/teaching continuum (see Figure I.1) more than you did previously, sometimes reflecting in action and at other times taking a careful step back to reflect on action. The skills, strategies and, most importantly, attitude you will develop will set you in the best possible direction to be the teacher you want to become.

Throughout this book the contributors have drawn upon their extensive experience of teaching and mentoring trainee teachers to present a wide range of case studies that you can adapt and use in your own classroom. The activities provided in each chapter will help you become actively engaged in strengthening your knowledge and understanding about the various skills and strategies that can be used for reflection. Each chapter concludes with a review of learning, and poses questions related to the content for you to reflect upon. Suggested responses to these self-assessment questions are included at the end of the book.

References

Ackermann, E. (1991) From decontextualized to situated knowledge: Revisiting Piaget's water-level experiment, In I. Harel and S. Papert (eds) *Constructionism*. Norwood, NJ: Ablex Publishing Corporation.

Arthur, J., Grainger, T. and Wray, D. (eds) (2006) *Learning to Teach in the Primary School*. London: Routledge.

Biggs, J. (1999) *Teaching for Quality Learning at University*. Buckingham: Open University Press.

Boud, D., Keogh, R. and Walker, D. (eds) (1985) *Reflection: Turning Experience into Learning*. London: Kogan Page.

Carr, M. (ed) (1996) *Motivation in Mathematics*. Cresskill, NJ: Hampton Press, cited in Goodchild, S. (2001) *Students' Goals: A Case Study of Activity in a Mathematics Classroom*. England: Hobbs the Printers.

Cinnamond, J.H. and Zimpher, N.L. (1990) Reflectivity as a function of community. In R.T. Clift, W.R. Houston and M.C. Pugach (eds) *Encouraging Reflective Practice in Education: An Analysis of Issues and Programs*. New York: Teachers College Press.

Christiansen, B. and Walther, G. (1986) Task and activity. In D. Christiansen, A.G. Howson and M. Otte (eds) *Perspectives on Mathematics Education*. Dordrecht: Reidel, cited in Goodchild, S. (2001) *Students' Goals: A Case Study of Activity in a Mathematics Classroom*. England: Hobbs the Printers.

Dewey, J. (1933) *How We Think: A Restatement of the Relation of Reflective Thinking to the Educative Process*. New York: D.C. Heath.

Eraut, M. (1996) Conceptual frameworks and historical development, In T. Plomp and D.P. Ely (eds.) *International Encyclopedia of Educational Technology*, 2nd ed. Oxford: Elsevier Science Ltd.

Goodchild, S. (2001) *Students' Goals: A Case Study of Activity in a Mathematics Classroom*. England: Hobbs the Printers.

Hinett, K. (2002) *Improving Reflective Practice in Legal Education*. UKLE.

Hoyles, C. (1985) What is the point of group discussion in mathematics? *Educational Studies In Mathematics*, 16: 205–14.

John-Steiner, V. and Mahn, H. (2003) Sociocultural contexts for teaching and learning. In W.M. Reynolds and G.E. Miller (eds) *Handbook of Psychology*. Hoboken, NJ: Wiley.

Kafai, Y.B. and Harel, I. (1991) Learning through consulting: When mathematical ideas, knowledge of programming and design, and playful discourse are intertwined. In I. Harel and S. Papert (eds) *Constructionism*. Norwood, NJ: Ablex Publishing Corporation.

King, P.M. and Kitchener, K.S. (2002) The reflective judgment model: Twenty years of research on epistemic cognition. In B.K. Hofer and P.R. Pintrich (eds) Personal Epistemology: The Psychology of Beliefs about Knowledge and Knowing. Mahwah, NJ: Lawrence Erlbaum.

Moon, J. (2001) *Reflection in Higher Education Learning*. PDP Working Paper 4. York: Higher Education Academy.

Race, P. (2004) *The Lecturer's Toolkit: A Practical Guide to Assessment, Learning and Teaching*. Abingdon: RoutledgeFalmer.

Schön, D. (1983) *The Reflective Practitioner: How Professionals Think in Action*, London: Temple Smith.

Smith, M.K. (1999) *Reflection*. Available at: www.infed.org/biblio/b-reflect.htm (accessed 4/1/12).

Sutton, A. (1980) Cited in John-Steiner, V. and Mahn, H. (2003) Sociolcultural contexts for teaching and learning. In Reynolds, W.M. and Miller, G.E. (eds) *Handbook of Psychology*. Hoboken, NJ: Wiley.

TLRP (online) *TLRP's Evidence-informed Pedagogic Principles*. Available at: http://www.tlrp.org/themes/themes/tenprinciples.html (accessed 9/1/12).

Wells, G. (1999) *Dialogic Inquiry: Toward a Sociocultural Practice and Theory of Education*. New York: Cambridge University Press.

Wood, D., Bruner, J.S. and Ross, G. (1979) The role of tutoring in problem solving. *Journal of Child Psychology and Psychiatry*, 17: 89–100.

Vygotsky, L.S. (1978) *Mind in Society: The Development of Higher Pyschological Processes*. Cambridge, MA: Harvard University Press.

Yackel, E. and Cobb, P. (1996) Sociomathematical norms, argumentation, and autonomy in mathematics. *Journal for Research in Mathematics Education*, 27(4): 458–77.

1. Children as reflective learners
Emma McVittie

Learning Outcomes

By the end of this chapter you will be able to:

- distinguish between being a reflective practitioner and how to encourage children to reflect;
- identify how reflection supports creative approaches to learning in the classroom;
- analyse what a reflective classroom looks like in practice.

What is reflection from a practitioner's perspective?

Theories about reflection tend to be fluid and not fact; they are amended and interpreted according to the needs of the researcher and the reader. To truly understand it you need to experience it and be inside it. As a general guide, reflection is about exploration and walking around things, the very thing we do a lot of in the classroom. It is like looking through a magnifying glass; some things are reduced in focus, others enhanced. As teachers, we encourage children to look at their experiences from different angles and increasingly ask children to examine their own learning. However, for children to become effective reflectors in your classroom, you yourself need a deep understanding of reflection in the classroom and how it can be used as a tool to aid skills such as analysis, evaluation and creativity, as well as vice versa.

Reflection is a process that is personal and erratic. We all reflect on things in different ways and that can depend on the context, emotion, level of involvement and our previous experiences in addition to many other variables. It does not follow a set pattern, hence it cannot be taught but only encouraged and supported under the right conditions in the classroom. Reflection is concerned with the process and not the product and many theorists put the process at the centre of their research by considering levels of reflection.

Activity

Consider how you reflect as an adult. Choose a recent event, such as a birthday, a journey, a shopping trip. Write down a reflection on this event and then answer the following questions.

- Is this just a broad description or have you included detail?
- Have you analysed the event, raised questions?
- Have you learned anything from this event?

Levels of reflection

Reflection is like appreciating a piece of art or literature and looking at the levels of meaning there. To effectively reflect in this way, children need a structured framework which guides them and helps you to plan for learning through reflection. The research focus below offers one such framework.

Research Focus

Hatton and Smith (1995) provide an academic construct of levels of reflection. Although the levels are hierarchical and indicate progression to deeper levels, they are not intended to be followed in a particular order, as you can enter and leave reflective activity at any level. The levels have been annotated here to focus on children reflecting. However, the original text has also been included in places as it is important that you as a teacher understand how reflection works for different audiences.

Descriptive writing
This can be done orally with children of any age individually, in groups or as a whole class. It is not reflective, it is simply describing an event, action or lesson. For example: Children in Key Stage 1, sitting on the carpet, are being asked: 'Can anyone tell me what you have been doing in our maths lesson today?'

Descriptive reflection
This is not only a description of an event, action or lesson but some attempt to provide reasons for how things went. For example, 'I found those sums easy because I used unifix.'

Dialogic reflection
'Demonstrates a "stepping back" from the events/actions leading to a different level of mulling about, discourse with self and exploring the experience, events, and actions using qualities of judgements and possible alternatives for explaining and hypothesising' (Hatton and Smith, 1995, p.48). For example: children thinking about *why* one prefers using unifix to help with their addition and someone else prefers using a number line; talking to each other about this.

Critical reflection
'Demonstrates an awareness that actions and events are not only located in, and explicable by, reference to multiple perspectives but are located in, and influenced by multiple historical, and socio-political contexts' (Hatton and Smith, 1995, p.49). For example, children realising that there are many reasons for their choice, such as what the teacher provided, how they learn best; what has influenced their choice – the school, class, friends; thinking about how others learn and even what other equipment children might use in various countries.

The tools of reflection

Bloom's taxonomy

In order to guide children in the varying levels of reflection, you need to support the development of some of the higher order thinking skills in the cognitive domain of Bloom's taxonomy (Bloom and Krathwohl, 1956). The model systematically classifies the processes of thinking and learning and was revised and updated by Anderson and Krathwohl in 2001. The revision renamed the skills and transposed the top two higher order skills. As both versions are used in education, both are detailed here (see Table 1.1).

Higher order thinking skills	Anderson and Krathwohl	Bloom and Krathwohl
	Creating	Evaluation
	Evaluating	Synthesis
	Analysing	Analysis
	Applying	Application
	Understanding	Comprehension
Lower order thinking skills	Remembering	Knowledge

Table 1.1: Thinking skills (Anderson and Krathwohl, 2001; Bloom and Krathwohl, 1956)

Understanding

To remember or have knowledge of a situation or event is not the same as understanding it. The two must go hand in hand for learning to take place. A good example of this is learning by rote: the knowledge is there but the reasoning and understanding may not be. Learning times tables is important but alongside this children must be taught how to manipulate numbers and understand them. Therefore understanding of this knowledge is essential.

These are useful terms to help you think about encouraging understanding alongside knowledge acquisition.

- Interpret
- Outline
- Discuss
- Explain
- Describe

Understanding has a key role to play, as children's reflection is concerned with exploration, thinking and questioning, which all have the potential to lead to increased comprehension.

Analysing

This is a key tool in reflection and can be taught in an appropriate way to any age group. Analysis of an event or aspect of an event may seem a rather academic term to use when discussing children's learning. However, this is only because of the academic context the word is usually placed in. By exploring what analysis means, you can identify activities that can help to develop this skill in children.

These are useful terms to help you think about analysis in the classroom.

- Examine
- Compare
- Contrast
- Explain
- Investigate
- Identify

Analysis features in each of Hatton and Smith's levels from 'descriptive reflection' onwards, increasing in depth at each stage. Day-to-day learning objectives will often have analytical elements, but to make reflective learning explicit children must have structured opportunities to develop these skills. If you are asking children to 'investigate' as part of their learning objective, then ensure your planning provides appropriate opportunities for investigative learning.

Activity

Look at the list of terms linked to analysing. Think about a potential activity for Key Stage 1 and Key Stage 2. Then write a series of questions that will help develop their skills of analysis and therefore deepen their reflection.

One example for the activity above is to think about 'comparing'. A Key Stage 1 class may be looking at a variety of art images and you could ask the question – How is *this* picture similar to *that* picture?

Evaluation

Evaluation is viewed by many as one of the easier skills despite its being ranked as one of the higher order processes in the taxonomy. The reason for this would appear to be the misunderstanding about what evaluation entails. It is more than having an opinion or stating what could be improved; it is concerned with making judgements and defending them with reference to set criteria and/or evidence.

These are useful terms to help you encourage the children to think about evaluation in the classroom.

- Justify
- Debate
- Assess
- Determine
- Judge

The use of evaluation in children's reflection links to Hatton and Smith's 'critical reflection' as demonstrated with the earlier example of why children may have a preference for particular resources to support their mathematics. 'Critical reflection' asks children to make judgements, justify the possible reasons and determine why certain choices are made. This can also include debates, presenting opinions/viewpoints and deciding on the criteria for judging a competition.

Creating

This skill links directly into creative thinking, discussed later in the chapter. Young children are better at synthesising or creating information and this needs further encouragement as children get older.

These are useful terms to help you think about how to encourage children to create in the classroom.

- Imagine
- Devise
- Create
- Compose
- Invent

Reflection involves looking at events from different perspectives and this is encouraged through using creative and open thinking. Examples of this skill include asking children to devise a new language or code to write a secret message, or to invent a machine for a task. At first glance these appear to be 'fun' activities but in order for children to succeed they will have to use their skills of comprehension, application and analysis first – which makes a seemingly 'fun' activity into quite a challenging one.

Primary-aged children reflecting

Young children are concerned with themselves and their needs; they think and act in a subjective manner. This way of thinking allows them to get to know themselves, their likes and dislikes, emotions and strengths. It is an innate process of reflection that often takes place subconsciously and enables children to adjust their perceptions and future reactions to experiences. As children develop they are taught to see situations and events from others' perspectives as well as their own – beginning the journey from a subjective to an objective frame of reference.

Reflection requires being honest in your own thinking and an ability to question your experiences and perspectives, which can lead to a greater understanding about a situation, alternative approaches and solutions to problems. The move from the subjective to the objective stance supports the reflective process but care must be taken not to confuse reflection with critical thinking, as this will discourage essential creativity and emotional engagement.

Research Focus: Internal and external dialogue as a means of reflection

For the purpose of this chapter internal dialogue is framed within the concept of reflection and in the educational sphere. Speech and talk were discussed in the Introduction and this research focus develops the notion.

There are two forms of dialogue: external and internal. Each can take many forms and be for a variety of purposes, including: incidental, conversational, analytical, evaluative, and emotional. An external dialogue is with another individual or group; an internal dialogue is a conversation with yourself, a place where decisions are made and choices evaluated. Hatton and Smith (1995) found that greater dialogic reflection was evident when students interacted with critical friends. Ballantyne and Packer (1995) indicated that students perceived one of the main weaknesses of journal writing to be its solitary nature. Internal dialogues can range from simple exchanges about whether your husband will notice if you buy another pair of shoes to more profound debates about where you stand in relation to a political or religious issue. These exchanges arise in everyone but some people engage with them on a more conscious level than others. This internal dialogue can be recognised and continued as an aid to decision-making or motivation, or it can be recognised but little value attached to it. This raises the question of the recognition and development of this dialogue and can lead down several pathways.

There are two aspects of internal dialogue. The primary internal aspect of dialogue can only be theorised about due to its intrinsic quality and personal dimension, as it is a spontaneous discourse that is only known to the individual. However, the secondary aspect involves the dialogue being recognised and formalised through reflection and the discourse begins to take place in a verbal or written manner.

Is reflection internal dialogue? No, but internal dialogue can be an aspect of reflection. It is the representation of this reflection on dialogue that allows it to be investigated. Writing is a representation of reflection; this representation is always a modified version and therefore deeper learning will take place. Dialogue is at the core of reflective practice – it enables us to walk around and explore issues without necessarily making a judgement.

Ways to support children in reflective dialogue

Remember that reflective dialogue is not just a discussion; it needs focus and planning to be an effective tool in the classroom. Internal dialogue is simply the internal conversations we all have on a daily basis, that usually accompany decision-making or experiences. If you think about children playing, working out a mathematics problem, painting or making things, they will talk to themselves to figure out the best course of action or how to do something – this is all internal dialogue, reflection. It is something that we take for granted and do in an almost unconscious manner. External dialogue involves sharing your thoughts and allowing others to comment on them. So how can we actively encourage children to reflect in this way in the classroom, rather than just leaving it to chance? The following suggestions aim to give you a foundation for using dialogue in a structured way. The key to the success of all these techniques is careful planning to facilitate reflection.

Using 'thinking' questions

How are these different from the questions posed to children on a daily basis in the classroom? All questioning links to learning in some form, whether recalling knowledge, checking understanding or clarifying an answer. Thinking questions are planned with a specific purpose in mind and that is to deepen children's learning through reflection; they are very rarely used in isolation. They often consist of a series of open questions which require children to think about the focus in a different way.

Examples of thinking questions:

- What would happen if . . .
- I wonder . . .
- What do you think about . . .
- In what way . . .
- Tell me about . . .
- What would you do . . .
- How can we . . .
- How did you . . .

Sharing pairs

This is a popular technique throughout education but it can become overused. So you need to ensure that you have a clear purpose for using sharing pairs and that it is employed effectively. Sharing pairs are usually, but not exclusively, used during whole class teaching to allow children time to think of ideas and answers before sharing with the teacher. These ideas should be prompted by 'thinking' questions.

Case Study: Why did Van Gogh paint sunflowers?

Andrew is a postgraduate primary student on his final teaching placement in the Summer term in a mixed Year 1/2 class. This is an edited transcript of the first art lesson in a series that looked at a variety of Van Gogh's paintings, focusing on the use of colour and what influenced his choices.

A version of Van Gogh's 'Sunflowers' is displayed on the interactive whiteboard and some calming music is playing in the background. The children are sitting on the carpet area.

→

The children are asked to look at the painting and think about it.

'Today we are going to think about why Van Gogh painted 'Sunflowers'. Have a look at the painting and think about one thing that you notice.'

The children are given one minute on an egg timer to do this.

'Now share what you have noticed with the person next to you.'

Again one minute on the egg timer.

'Did you notice some of the same things as your partner? Did you notice something different from your partner?'

Children are now asked to share what they have noticed with the whole class.

'Now I want you to think about what you like about the "Sunflowers".'

Pause.

'Why do you like this?'

One minute.

'Now share with the person next to you.'

One minute.

'Did you agree with your partner?'

Children are now asked to share with the class what their partner liked and why.

'Why do you think he painted sunflowers and not another flower, or a hillside?'

One minute.

'Share with the person next to you'

One minute.

The children are grouped into four with their sharing partner at their tables.

'Now share all your ideas in your group about why Van Gogh might have painted sunflowers and not another flower or a hillside.'

Andrew waves his fingers in the air and the children gradually stop their discussions and copy him. Once the children are quiet and looking:

'I'm going to tell you why Van Gogh painted the sunflowers. It was to decorate a room in his house ready for a friend visiting. Think about what you would paint to welcome a friend.'

One minute.

'Share your ideas about what you would paint with your partner.'

→

> Andrew walked around the class and asked the children about their ideas. He encouraged them to ask questions of each other to help them develop their ideas further.
>
> Children got out their reflective journals and could write or draw what they would paint for a friend visiting and why.

As you can see, sharing pairs emulates a common class discussion but by planning the reflective questions and allowing children opportunities to share and reflect on their own and others' thoughts, you are encouraging deeper learning. This learning is further developed by children representing their reflections in some way.

Stop, share and compare

This technique is a natural progression from sharing pairs for Key Stage 2 children. Once the pupils gain confidence in their reflections, this activity becomes a valuable learning opportunity. 'Stop, share, compare' can be used as a group or whole class technique, providing that the children are all working on the same topic or concept. Although the formula is very simple, once again care must be taken to structure the process.

Stop!

Once the children have had time to engage with their tasks, stop the group/class with your preferred method (hands in the air, fiddly fingers, etc.). The 'stop' should be planned for a specific point in your lesson, until you become comfortable with the reflective questioning. Once you feel confident then a 'stop' may be prompted by a pupil's question, or a misconception that you notice a number of children are having difficulty with.

Share

When the children have stopped their work, you raise a 'thinking question' linked to what the children are working on – this may be to clarify or extend their learning. Ask them to take a minute to think about it. Now ask children to share their reflections on this with you/the class.

Compare

Children have the opportunity to talk about their thoughts on their tables for one minute.

'Why?' wall

Reflection is concerned with walking around an event or situation. This exploration involves questioning and wondering. Sometimes there will be questions that children feel they cannot voice, for a variety of reasons. The purpose of a 'Why?' wall is to encourage children to submit questions anonymously for reflection, focused on a chosen topic that is being studied in that half term/term.

You will need:

- A large piece of coloured card to act as the wall. This can be decorated by the children to give them ownership or you can use a ready-made notice board.
- Pieces of coloured paper or sticky notes for children to write their questions/thoughts on. These can be made from laminated card so dry wipe pens can be used and they can be stuck on the wall with Velcro attachments.
- Pens/pencils.

Depending on your class, you can organise use of the wall in a number of different ways:

- *Open access*: anyone can write at any time.
- *Groups*: small groups will have a set day and time where support will be available if needed. This could happen as part of the topic lesson each week.
- *Group days*: groups of five or six children will have access on a particular day.

Suggested stimuli for the 'Why?' wall:

- From caterpillar to butterfly
- Stars and planets
- A piece of artwork, poem, book or music
- An aspect of nature – looking at changing seasons or plant growth
- A mathematics concept
- Current global or historical events
- Questions about beliefs
- How things work – design technology

The responses to the questions and thoughts can spark class reflective dialogue throughout the period of the topic. As the teacher, you could also post possible answers, or pose your own questions in response to children's thoughts. Older children may also be able to contribute in this way once the process is established.

Journals

In Chapter 8 Helen Davenport writes about the use of reflective journals in your own professional and academic practice. However, they can also be used with children. Reflective journals vary greatly in their effectiveness (Dart et al, 1998; Canning, 1991; Ghaye and Ghaye, 1998). It is not simply providing children, or even adults, with a blank page and asking them to 'reflect' on a particular situation or event. The tools discussed earlier in the chapter can be utilised to a greater extent here, and children must have had some practice with other reflective techniques before they embark on journals. The most important point to remember about journals is that reflections do not have to be in written form only. There are many ways of communicating thoughts and feelings, including pictures, diagrams, notes, doodles and colour.

However, children must be guided in using the media they choose to make sure that it is suitable and appropriate.

Journal guidance

Children must have ownership of their journals so they feel they *want* to use them rather than making it an onerous task. One effective way to do this is to ask children to design their own journal as part of a project. In this way, they can personalise their paper and the cover of the journal and are more likely to use it freely to record valuable reflections. If this is not possible then each child should be given a book that they can personalise at home/school. When you begin using journals in the class, plan for their use in a topic or scheme of work and allow time for the children to get used to this way of working. Use 'thinking questions' to structure responses, in addition to the techniques mentioned previously to encourage reflective thinking. Moon (2006) suggests using a double-entry technique, which can be used to aid varying outcomes of reflection such as reflection on the learning from writing a journal, and reflection on the process and re-reading. Double entry can be done by writing on one side of the page and leaving the other side for further reflections.

A potential obstacle when using journals can be the issue of privacy. If you want to encourage children to reflect honestly then the journals need to remain private unless an individual chooses to share any part of it with a friend or an adult – if the journals are collected in or judged by the teacher then children will record what they consider is 'correct' or what they think the teacher wants to see. According to Salisbury (1994) the fact that the reflections are to be viewed by a tutor and possibly assessed can result in students writing what they think will please the tutor. This raises a question about the purpose of a journal – unlike other pieces of written work, a reflective journal is not an assessment tool. For a teacher, and indeed anyone involved in education, this can feel a little uncomfortable. Reflection is about the learning that happens as a consequence of the process and not about the recorded reflection itself. Boud et al (1985) reported that the use of reflection 'facilitated my ability to share the experience which I recorded in it. It allows one to share objectively and fruitfully – once you've written something down – one views it more clearly. Once it's brought out into the open it loses its power.'

An alternative to individual journals is a class journal – rather like a visitors' book in a holiday cottage. The reflections are visible to others, though they still remain anonymous. All the children can contribute by using pieces of paper to record their reflections, which are then glued into the journal along with the question that was posed. The class journal has the advantage of giving the teacher an overview of the thoughts and feelings of the class while still retaining some element of privacy. For younger children a period of time each week could be set aside for reflection. This can include playing calming music, reflecting as a class, and then reflecting in groups either for an individual or class journal. Contributions may be written by an adult, or children can produce some writing or a drawing independently which they can then talk about and share with an older child or adult.

Case Study: Using reflective journals to think about Goldilocks

A class of mixed Key Stage 2 children are examining fairy tales from different perspectives which will culminate in writing play scripts and using drama. The teacher has been using reflective techniques with the class and has decided to move on to use reflective journals. The lesson begins with the teacher telling the story of Goldilocks and the Three Bears, with the children all sitting in a circle in the hall. It is told rather than read, to create an atmosphere and allow the children to picture the images in their heads. Some children close their eyes and others even react to parts of the story with 'Bleurr' when Goldilocks eats some cold porridge. Throughout the storytelling, the teacher uses prompts to help the children think about the story in more detail.

The reflective question is: 'Can you describe where you think the three bears lived?' Different answers are given, such as 'cottage', 'cave', 'forest'. The teacher then asks the children to close their eyes and go back to this place: 'How does it feel to be there?' Responses vary: 'cold and damp', 'gloomy', 'warm and 'cosy'.

They discuss other elements, such as: What can you see in this place? What are the chairs made from? What does the porridge smell like? Then the teacher plays some music and the children are led back to the classroom to begin their journals.

The children are encouraged to speak to a partner about how they would like to reflect on this question and to think about what materials they might need.

The children settle and begin their reflections. Some are writing, others are drawing and labelling and one or two sit with their eyes closed for a moment before they start. Bethany's and Robert's journal entries show how the children are being guided to do descriptive reflection and demonstrate their understanding.

Figure 1.1: Bethany's (aged 8) response to where the three bears lived

→

Bethany was able to talk very clearly about what each part of her reflection was and why she had done it in that way. It also related to her own life as she said that they went out to collect wood for the fire at home:

> *Well, I thought of a cottage because fairy tales have cottages in woods and it has to be big for the bears to fit in so I wrote it in big writing. I put fires there because it is all warm and cosy inside. I tried to write it in a love heart because you can feel warm and cosy inside too, but it went a bit wrong.*

Other children responded in different ways. Robert thought about it in a very practical way:

> *Bears live in caves and it's very dark and gloomy in there. Daddy Bear has made the cave and chiselled the furniture. Oh, and the cave leaks too.*

The teacher used many reflective techniques to deepen the children's learning and tried to relate the thinking questions to higher order thinking skills. In the final reflective lesson children composed music for the story, which was later used in the performance of their plays.

Review – what's new?

This is based on plenary sessions but has a more reflective focus. It is not confined to the end of a lesson and can be more beneficial if used at various points throughout. Once again, planning is imperative to the success of this technique. There will be various points in your lessons when key learning takes place, although the children may not be aware of this happening. 'Review – what's new?' simply gives you the opportunity to make this learning explicit.

Stop the children at a specific point and ask them to share what they have learnt. This can be recorded in a variety of ways:

- as a group in a shared journal;
- individually;
- collated on a class sheet and scribed by the teacher.

The act of consciously sharing their learning will reinforce it and allow them to question and develop it. It also serves as a prompt to those who may need it and as an assessment tool for the teacher.

Activity

Think about a lesson you have taught. Which of the above reflective dialogue techniques could you have used and why? What impact might these have had on the children's learning if you had used them in the lesson?

How reflection supports creative learning approaches in the classroom

Once you begin to regularly focus on structuring and supporting children's reflections, you will find that it opens many doors for your teaching and learning. Giving time and space to reflection can also lead to an increased creative approach and opportunities for creative responses. Creativity is yet another term, like reflection, that has a multitude of definitions, and advice is everywhere on how to be 'creative'. The most common definition of creativity in relation to education is from the National Advisory Committee on Creative and Cultural Education (1999, p.29): 'Imaginative activity fashioned so as to produce outcomes that are both original and of value'.

People tend to get fixated on the words 'original and of value' to the extent where it becomes increasingly difficult to be creative in any form. However, generally speaking, an individual's thoughts are original to them and certainly of value. In the case of children, they are far more likely to generate original ideas when they are scaffolded by reflective techniques. This can clearly be seen in the 'Goldilocks' case study.

In addition to the whole debate about definitions, there are two ways to define creativity: you can think and learn in a creative way, or you can demonstrate your learning through creative responses. Craft (2000) talks of 'possibility thinking' which can be supported through creative ways of learning and further enhanced by reflective techniques. 'Possibility thinking' is thinking with no boundaries, looking at the 'possible' solutions and not just the 'probable': 'A possibility thinker will answer a question with further questions – leading them into new ways of thinking about the world around them' (Craft, 2000, p.6).

An interesting activity to encourage children's creative and reflective skills is to choose an everyday object, such as a peg. Now ask the children, in groups, to think of five obvious ways to use the object, including what it was designed for. Then to think of a further five ways, and a further five, until their suggestions become 'possibilities' rather than 'probabilities'. For example, 'Take the peg apart and use them as skis for a mouse' (child aged 6), or 'use them as chopsticks' (child aged 10). Follow this by using dialogic and/or analytical reflection to consider all the suggestions, justifying and modifying ideas and identifying their limitations.

The latter definition links directly to reflection as you are encouraging children to represent their reflections in a variety of ways. The tools and levels of reflection also aid creative thinking and creative responses through questioning, looking at various perspectives and encouraging internal and external dialogue with others.

Research Focus: The lily-pad model

The lily-pad model is an adaptation of Hatton and Smith's (1995) levels of reflection and is based on action research by McVittie (2009). As touched upon earlier, reflection is a process but it is not one that can easily be put into a hierarchical diagram and followed. The lily-pad model is a teaching model of reflective activity to be used as a tool for educationalists to explore how reflection may look in their context and how to deepen children's experience of it through structured techniques. Used in conjunction with the suggested approaches in this chapter, it provides an accessible starting point.

- *Recall reflection*: a simple description of an experience which mainly recalls facts.
- *Context-led reflection*: linking previous learning to the current context.
  Have I experienced this before?
  What was it like?
  Can it help me here?
- *Analytical reflection*: looking at others' experiences and ideas.
  Does this help my understanding?
  Stop, Share, Compare.
- *Critical reflection*: looking beyond myself.
  Using books, internet-based resources, historical literature to explore similar situations.
- *Active reflection*: returning to reflections and applying learning to a new situation.
  Using journals to reflect on reflections.
  Double-entry journals.

An important issue to raise is the relationship between critical thinking and reflection. Although they can overlap and indeed have characteristics in common, critical thinking is more towards the development of a judgement while reflection is about exploration and walking around things (Moon, 2008).

Activity

Using the lily-pad model as a reference, how could you plan for children to progress from analytical reflection to critical reflection?

Reflection and creativity in action

An example from the curriculum might be: using music as a creative medium and asking children to review the lyrics using thinking questions in their journals and finally produce a creative response to a set question. An excellent starting point for using music in this way can be found in Webster (2010), who demonstrates a variety of creative approaches to Religious

Education in the classroom. The following activity was adapted from Webster (2010, p.64) for use in CPD and consequently taken successfully into primary schools.

Music: 'If God Was One of Us' (lyrics from www.lyricsondemand.com) by Joan Osbourne.

Reflective techniques used: Thinking questions, sharing pairs, 'Why?' wall, reflective journals.

Suggested progression: Listen to the song several times over a set period, perhaps with eyes closed to help children create pictures in their minds. Sometimes the song could be followed with a whole class discussion about what they like and dislike about the song, followed by some *sharing pairs* and 'descriptive reflection' in their *journal*.

- How do the instruments and/or tempo create the mood of the song?
- If you changed the instruments/tempo, would it change the mood of the song?

Look in detail at the lyrics in a literacy lesson using *thinking questions* to prompt discussion about the writer's view of God. There are some great ideas for questions at: www.jesusonthetube.co.uk/.

- 'What if God was one of us' – *What do you think this means?*
- 'Just a slob like one of us' – *Why would God be a slob? How may this have happened?*
- 'Just a stranger on the bus' – *Would you sit next to God? What would you say?*
- 'Trying to make his way home' – *Where is home?*

Children select a question to respond to in their journals. Make time for sharing if children choose to at this point.

Using a *'Why?' wall*, pick out lyrics to provoke thinking and reflection, such as: What would you ask God if you had just one question?

Listen again to the song, this time with the lyrics on view for those who can read them.

Focus on the line: 'He's trying to make his way home back up to heaven all alone.' Ask the question: *Would God have been alone?* Use *sharing pairs* followed by *journals* after discussion.

Finally, ask children to imagine (link to Bloom's most complex thinking skill) if God/Jesus lived in their town/village/street. Then ask them to describe God's characteristics (children can draw if appropriate to their religious beliefs). Why would God be like that? Would God's character be influenced by your town/area?

Use *sharing pairs* to discuss their thoughts so far. Then think about how/if listening to others' ideas makes you consider adapting your own, using *journals*.

Activity

Consider how reflection and creativity are inextricably linked. The best platform for this combination is through cross-curricular learning. The previous example combined music and RE; another example could be reflecting on history through a creative PE lesson. Experiment with combinations of subjects and topics to create an outline for a series of lessons that detail:

- the tasks;
- the key 'thinking questions';
- reflective techniques used;
- how they link to the lily-pad model.

A reflective classroom in practice

Difficulties associated with transferring theory into a practical classroom situation

Gustafson and Bennett (1999) identified 11 variables that can restrict effective reflection. These can be grouped into three areas: the learner, the environment and the task.

The learner

The learner is central to reflection and, as stated at the beginning of the chapter, reflection is personal and therefore each child will approach it in their own way. Some will have an innate ability to reflect while others will find it more difficult and will need further support. The biggest obstacle to this in a classroom with around 30 children is the time needed to consistently develop children's skills. Try to build reflection into your timetable and have separate plans for it, to begin with, until you are practised enough to include it as part of your lessons. Even when reflection is planned for, it may not be successful. Children must be motivated to engage with reflection, whether it be intrinsic or extrinsic. Feather (1982) discussed the value theory of motivation – the need to value the outcome and expect success in achieving it. If either one of these is not valued then there will be no motivated activity. This is especially true in the early stages of learning.

The environment

What the classroom feels like is just as important as what happens in it. By setting up the classroom to encourage reflection, you are encouraging learning in general. Areas to consider (Bandura, 1977):

- *The layout* – is it easy to work in sharing pairs? Can children easily move around the classroom? Is there a quiet area for children to reflect for the class journal? Can you create a quiet environment with music for reflective times?
- *Displays* – is there an appropriate area for a 'Why?' wall and other interactive resources?
- *Equipment* – can children access materials for their reflective journals?
- *Music* – this is a good way of creating a calming atmosphere when reflecting on things that are personal or sensitive.

- *The social environment* – create an accepting and caring ethos that promotes interpersonal interaction.

The task

What you are asking the children to do will impact on the quality of reflections. Reflections can be categorised into three types: reacting, elaborating and contemplating (Surbeck et al, 1991). Make sure you are clear what you are asking of them so that you know how best to support their learning.

How you ask children to reflect will influence their responses. Some children will love the freedom of the journal whereas others will find they need more input and structure. The same can be said of the techniques that use partners or sharing with others – be aware that not every child will benefit from all the techniques.

Feedback is also important. You may not be marking their reflection but acknowledging that it is happening and commenting on what children share is vital to nurture the environment for reflection.

Activity
Create a reflective classroom
If you could set up your classroom in any way you wanted to and money was no object, what would it look like? Think about the reflective environment and the kind of space and resources you would need to encourage deep reflection and learning. How does this activity reflect your understanding of deep reflection and learning in the classroom?

Simple reflective activities for the classroom

These activities can be used with all primary-aged children to get you started using reflective thinking with children.

Picture plenary
Give the children a piece of paper and ask them to draw pictures to represent how they would mark their understanding in the lesson – no words allowed!

Dear Me...
The children write to themselves on a postcard about their learning. This could be about any subject you like but could include: something they liked; or something they want to improve. This can be written, scribed or done with pictures.

Team talk

This is used to encourage children to reflect on working in a team. Individually they think about one item under each heading. The headings are displayed on a large piece of paper, where the children will record their thoughts together. For example:

- Plus points
- Minus points
- Interesting points.

Ups and downs

This can be done individually or in groups. Children record the ups and downs of the lesson or topic on a graph. The ups and downs can illustrate excitement, achievement, engagement with the task, enjoyment, understanding, uncertainty, etc.

Score!

Arrange a line on the floor with numbers on it from 0 to 10. Either during or after a lesson or topic, ask the children to stand on the appropriate number on the line in response to questions asked by the teacher, to score their learning and understanding.

Learning Outcomes Review

This chapter began by analysing reflection from a practitioner's perspective, including the theory that surrounds this. It was suggested that to be able to encourage children to reflect, the practitioner needed to experience it and be inside it. Specific skills and techniques were introduced to link the theory and practice together and scaffold the use of dialogue to deepen learning. The relationship between reflection and creativity was explored using a cross-curricular example and a suggested teaching framework was proposed in the form of the lily-pad model. Finally the difficulties associated with a reflective classroom in practice were examined which looked at the learner, the task and the environment and how to overcome these difficulties.

Self-assessment questions
1. Can you define what reflection looks like for a practitioner and for a child?
2. What are the different levels of reflection?
3. How can you use Bloom's higher order thinking skills to support children's reflection?
4. How can you support children's reflective dialogue in the classroom?
5. What is the relationship between reflection and creativity?
6. What difficulties may you face when putting theory into practice and how can these be overcome?

Further Reading

Epstein, A.S. (2003) How planning and reflection develop young children's thinking skills. *Young Children*, 58(5): 28–36.

Hatton, N. and Smith, D. (1995) Reflection in teacher education: Towards definition and implementation. *Teaching and Teacher Education*, 11(1): 33–49. Cited in Bain et al (1999).

Hong, S.B. and Broderick, J.T. (2003) Instant video revisiting for reflection: Extending the learning of children and teachers. *Early Childhood Research & Practice: An Internet Journal on the Development, Care, and Education of Young Children*, Spring 2003.

Moon, J.A. (2006) *Learning Journals: A Handbook of Reflective Practice and Professional Development*, 2nd ed. London: Routledge.

References

Anderson, L.W. and Krathwohl, D.R. (eds) (2001) *A Taxonomy for Learning, Teaching, and Assessing: A Revision of Bloom's Taxonomy of Educational Objectives*. New York: Longman.

Bain, J., Ballantyne, R., Packer, J. and Mills, C. (1999). Using journal writing to enhance student teachers reflectivity during field experience placements. *Teachers and Teaching: Theory and Practice*, 5(1): 51–73.

Ballantyne, R. and Packer J. (1995) *Making Connections: Using Student Journals as a Teaching/Learning Aid*. Canberra, ACT: Higher Education Research and Development Society of Australasia.

Bandura, A. (1977) *Social Learning Theory*. New York: General Learning Press.

Bloom, B.S. and Krathwohl, D.R. (1956) *Taxonomy of Educational Objectives: The Classification of Educational Goals, by a committee of college and university examiners. Handbook I: Cognitive Domain*. New York: Longmans, Green.

Boud, D., Keogh, R. and Walker, D. (1985) *Reflection: Turning Experience into Learning*, London: Kogan Page.

Canning, C. (1991) What the teachers say about reflection. *Educational Leadership*, March.

Craft, A. (2000) *Creativity Across the Primary Curriculum*. Abingdon: Routledge.

Dart, B., Boulton-Lewis, G., Brownlee, J. and McCrindle, A. (1998) Change in knowledge of learning and teaching through journal-writing, *Research Papers in Education*, 13 (3): 291–318.

Feather, N. (ed) (1982) *Expectations and Actions*. Hillsdale, NJ: Erlbaum.

Ghaye, A. and Ghaye, K. (1998) *Teaching and Learning Through Critical Reflective Practice*. London: David Fulton.

Ghaye, A. and Lillyman, S. (1997) *Learning Journals and Critical Incidents*. Dinton: Quay Books.

Gustafson, K. and Bennett, W. (1999) Issues and difficulties in promoting learner reflection: Results from a three year study. Available at: www.http://it.coe.uga.edu/-kgustafs/document/promoting.html (retrieved 12/9/2008).

Hatton, N. and Smith, D. (1995). Reflection in teacher education: Towards definition and implementation. *Teaching and Teacher Education*, 11(1): 33–49. Cited in Bain et al (1999).

McVittie, E. (2009) Talking to Yourself in RE. *Association of University Lecturers in Religion and Education: Religion, Education and Dialogue*. University of Exeter, 20–21 July. Unpublished conference paper.

Moon, J.A. (2006) *Learning Journals: A Handbook of Reflective Practice and Professional Development*, 2nd ed. London: Routledge.

Moon, J.A. (2008) Seminar on Reflective Learning [personal notes].

NACCCE (1999) *All Our Futures: Creativity, Culture and Education*. London: NACCCE.

Salisbury, J. (1994). *Becoming Qualified: An Ethnography of a Post-experience Teacher Training Course*. PhD thesis, University College of Wales: Cardiff. Cited in Moon (2006).

Surbeck, E., Han, E.P. and Moyer, J. (1991) Assessing reflective responses in journals. *Educational Leadership*, March: 25–7.

Webster, M. (2010) *Creative Approaches to Teaching Primary RE*. Essex: Pearson.

2. Trainees and teachers as reflective learners

Alice Hansen

Learning Outcomes

By the end of this chapter you will have developed your understanding of how 'reflective practice' can:

- have a significant number of positive effects on your learning;
- improve your teaching and your academic work;
- be informal, formal, non-assessed or assessed and that each method has a different function.

Introduction

In the Introduction (see pages 1-10) you will have read about reflection and how the notion of reflective practice can be conceived within learning and teaching. This chapter explains why being a reflective trainee teacher, and subsequently a reflective teacher, is such a critical component of your role. It is my intention that if you already consider yourself to be a reflective trainee teacher, your understanding will be enhanced and you will continue to see the importance of being a reflective learner. If you are less convinced about the place of reflective practice in teaching, I hope that this chapter will help you to see that there are genuine benefits for embracing the notion of reflective learning and teaching.

Activity

During your course you may or may not have been convinced of the reasons why it is useful to be reflective in your work. Do you see it as an integrated core component of your job as a trainee teacher, or do you see it as an add-on? What role models do you have when it comes to reflective practice?

Note down your genuine thoughts, feelings and ideas about 'reflective practice' in the classroom and in your academic work. You may share these with a peer or tutor, or keep them to yourself. You will be asked to return to your notes at the end of this chapter.

As stated in the Introduction, 'reflection' is a difficult concept to define. However, identifying its impact is easier. McGill and Brockbank (1998) wrote a text for higher education tutors that identified a number purposes for reflection. Although the book has a focus much broader than initial teacher training, the purposes will resonate with your teacher training courses regardless of the route you are on. The purposes will be referred to throughout this chapter and book, and they include the following.

- Recording an experience
- Facilitating learning from an experience
- Supporting professional and academic understanding
- Developing critical thinking
- Encouraging the ability to think metacognitively
- Enhancing ownership of learning
- Developing evaluative skills
- Enhancing problem-solving skills
- Providing self-empowerment
- Supporting behaviour and feelings
- Enhancing creativity
- Improving writing
- Improving communication
- Enhancing interaction with others
- Supporting assignments

This chapter focuses on the impact that reflective learning will have on your own role as a teacher and in your academic study. Both of these elements are essential for your own professional and academic growth.

It is important to remember that although at times an artificial divide has been created in order to structure this chapter, in your own work the division will be blurred. After all, you may find yourself reflecting on a critical incident in the classroom and using this to inform an assignment, which in turn may provide a theoretical construct for you to act more effectively in a similar situation in the future.

Why should I be a reflective practitioner?

Beaty (1997, p.8) reminds us why reflective practice should be core to your work as a professional, academic trainee teacher and throughout your career.

> *Reflective practice is important to the development of all professionals because it enables us to learn from experience. Although we all learn from experience, more and more experience does not guarantee more and more learning. 20 years of teaching may not equate to 20 years of learning about teaching but may be only one year repeated 20 times. There are many times when our normal reactions to events are insufficient*

themselves to encourage reflection. We should not rely solely on our natural process of reflecting on experience, but actively seek ways to ensure that reflection itself becomes a habit, ensuring our continuing development as a professional teacher in higher education.

Beaty very clearly shows that one of the advantages of being reflective is that it is a mechanism for improving what you do as a teacher. Have you been on a placement where you have seen a teacher who has had 20 years of teaching experience, but who does not appear to have moved on in their own learning in that time as much as another teacher who may have had fewer years teaching? Remember, do not fall into the trap of assuming that older teachers are not reflective practitioners. Experienced teachers often develop ways of being reflective learners that are nearly invisible to the untrained eye!

The research focus below introduces the four stages of competence as a learning theory. It is offered here as a way of thinking about your own professional development and the role that reflection has within it.

Research Focus: The four stages of competence

The four stages of competence is a learning theory model. Its origins are unclear, with some (incorrectly) referencing Maslow in 1940 and others claiming Burch in the 1970s (www.gordontraining.com/free-workplace-articles/learning-a-new-skill-is-easier-said-than-done/). Regardless of its origins, it enjoys a worldwide appeal in a wide range of disciplines.

Essentially, the model suggests that there are four stages of competence that any learner will go through to learn a skill. These are:

1. Unconscious incompetence (you are unaware of what you do not yet know).

2. Conscious incompetence (you are aware there is something you do not know and you need to learn it).

3. Conscious competence (you are aware of what you are learning);.

4. Unconscious incompetence (you have learned the skill and do not need to think about it as you carry it out).

A search on Google Images will provide you with a plethora of models for how the stages might be represented. The stages are often shown with stage 1 as the beginning and stage 4 as the end point or goal, displayed as a ladder, steps, or a linear process. Others show the stages as a cycle, where there is no end point. I challenge both of these types of model because they imply that learning is simple and linear. Figure 2.1 shows my own interpretation of the model for a teaching-based context. Critical incidents are used to describe events or changes of circumstance that may cause a trainee/teacher to revert to an earlier level of competence. The case study that follows demonstrates the model in practice.

→

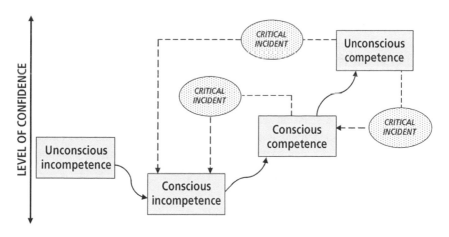

Figure 2.1: Four stages of competence for teaching

Case Study: Harry learns behaviour management again, and again, and again

In this case study you will see the four stages of competence in practice when we follow Harry through his one-year PGCE course, containing two long placements, and into his first year of teaching. You will see how his reflection on behaviour management is a longitudinal process in this case, and can be categorised using the four stages of competence.

Harry's experience

Prior to the PGCE course
Harry had observed two different teachers in different schools prior to beginning the course and concluded that the classes were 'well behaved' and that behaviour management was a straightforward aspect of being a teacher.

During first placement
Week 1: Harry thinks that he has been placed in an 'easy' Year 2 class because the children are well behaved for the class teacher. Towards the end of the first week he works with a group of children using his own lesson plan. Despite his best efforts to manage their behaviour, two children talk to each

The four stages of competence in practice

Harry is unconsciously incompetent about behaviour strategies at this point.

Harry has become aware that behaviour management is more difficult than he had assumed! He has now entered the stage of conscious incompetence about behaviour strategies.

→

35

other for the duration of the 20-minute task and achieve little, one child flicks pieces of eraser at others in the class with his ruler and another sits making the hole in her school sweater larger.

Weeks 2–3: After discussion with his mentor and reading about behaviour management, Harry starts to use a number of strategies and begins to manage the children's behaviour effectively.

Harry has become consciously competent in a limited number of behaviour management strategies.

Weeks 4–5: In his final weeks of placement, Harry begins to relax. He is starting to use some strategies (e.g. 'I like the way you are looking at me to show me you are listening') without thinking about it. Harry is enjoying working with the class and feels his behaviour management strategies are working well.

At times, Harry is already demonstrating an unconscious competence around some of the behaviour management strategies he has been using.

During second (final) placement
Weeks 1–2: Harry did not identify behaviour management as a target going into this placement. He felt confident in his abilities by the time he left his first placement class. However, he soon finds some behaviour management strategies not working to the same effect. Through his own reflection and discussion with his mentor he recognises a number of reasons for this including:

Harry has become aware again that behaviour management is more difficult and complex than he had assumed! In this new context he has re-entered the stage of conscious incompetence.

- A different age group requires different strategies
- Harry was too casual in his approach to the children when he started
- Harry tried to implement too many new approaches at once

Weeks 3–8: Harry learns quickly from the difficulties he had at the start of his placement and progresses well by broadening his repertoire of effective strategies to use with this age group.

Harry's competence evolves from the stage of conscious incompetence into conscious competence. Towards the end he operates within unconscious incompetence for most of the time.

→

Entering his first teaching post

In preparation for his new teaching job in another year group new to him, Harry spends some time observing the class he is due to teach in September just before their summer vacation. He makes notes of the behaviour management strategies that the class teacher uses and talks to her about these strategies. He also asks about some of the children that he will be teaching and asks the class teacher if she has any advice for him about how best to manage their behaviour given their particular needs.

Harry is aware of the situation he found himself in during the beginning of his final placement. He feels a level conscious incompetence once again.

Harry follows the school policy about behaviour and on the first day spends a lesson talking with the children about the school rules and his expectations of their behaviour. The class and school rules are displayed on the wall. Harry explains the sanctions for breaking the rules. During the first month, Harry ensures that he consistently applies the sanctions and uses a lot of praise to demonstrate how he expects the children to behave in the class.

Harry's feeling of conscious incompetence is ill founded and it is clear from his preparation and early days in school that he is operating at a conscious competence level. As the year progresses, Harry no longer thinks about the everyday behaviour management strategies he is using (unconscious competence) and only reverts to earlier stages when events force him to reassess his knowledge and understanding.

The case study shows how learning a skill or set of skills is not straightforward. The Introduction identified how learning is contextual and, particularly in teaching, is dependent on a significant number of factors. Many of the factors may be out of your control. It is essential to remember that although the model in Figure 2.1 identifies 'critical incidents' as a driver for moving to previous levels of competence, a critical incident may not be a terrible thing to happen to you. Harry, in the case study above, took the opportunity of observing his new class to ensure that he was clear on the behaviour management strategies the children were used to following. Here, the 'critical incident' was his visit to the new class.

A focus on you or the children?

It is also clear from the case study that Harry used reflection as a tool to consider what caused the unacceptable behaviour of the children on his second placement. With his mentor, he reflected on his own teaching behaviour and talked about how that had impacted upon the behaviour of the children in his placement classroom.

The activity below asks you to think about how reflecting on children's behaviour can provide a meaningful insight into children and their lives.

Activity
Reflecting on the impact you have in a classroom

This activity is designed to encourage you to think about the impact that reflecting on what drives children to behave in a certain way can have on your attitude towards them and the way that you ensure appropriate learning opportunities happen for them. Think about the following comments.

Teacher A
1. He's a lazy child, he'll never get the work done in a lesson.
2. She has no hope of doing her homework when you think of the situation she is living in at home.
3. They can't sit together because they always go off-task.

Teacher B
1. James worries about his spelling and so he is sometimes slow to put his ideas on paper.
2. Sometimes Melany will ask you if she can take a pencil home to do her homework. It is OK for her to do that and it doesn't matter if it isn't returned.
3. Maisha and Jo need to be given a task that really gets them interested. Then they'll stick at it for ages.

Have you met teachers who make comments like those above? Now, if you haven't already, pair the first statements from each teacher, then the next two and finally the last two. Can you see that they are comments about the same children by different teachers?

Which teacher would you prefer to undertake a placement with? Which teacher would you have preferred to have had as a child? Which classroom would you like your own children to learn and develop in? Which teacher would you like as a colleague in your first year of teaching?
To what extent do you think Teacher A and Teacher B are reflective practitioners? Why?

A little time taken to reflect upon the reasons why a child behaved in a certain way, or carried out a task, or attained a certain level, can certainly impact upon how you understand them and how you approach your planning of their learning.

You may have also noted that you felt a difference in attitude towards each of the teachers who made the statements, or towards the children being talked about. When I carried out this activity, I found myself saddened that a teacher (A) could be so dismissive and superficially judgemental of the children in the class. There appears no deeper desire to reflect on why those children – James, Melany, Maisha and Jo – behave in certain ways, and instead rest the blame for their behaviour with them. It seems to me that Teacher A assumes that teaching is about themselves, whereas Teacher B focuses on the children and their development. What expectations do you have about teaching and being a teacher? Which teacher would you prefer to be like?

Your expectations in the workplace can have a significant impact on the way you approach a situation and learn from it. Expectations are often related to relationships. Sometimes this is referred to as a psychological contract and if one or more of the parties involved feel that the contract has been breached then there is often a negative response (Conway and Briner, 2005; Cullinane and Dundon, 2006). The following section explores your expectations of being a trainee teacher.

Trainees' and tutors' course expectations

Adrian Copping explains in Chapter 3 that your training course has been carefully validated in order to offer the greatest opportunity for reflective learning to happen. However, this can cause a tension if your expectations of the learning opportunities you will experience are different from the intentions of your tutors (Conway and Briner, 2005; Cullinane and Dundon, 2006). Carry out the activity below to explore this idea further.

Activity
Select the statements in Table 2.1 that closely match your expectations of your initial teacher training course.

As a student on an academic course I . . .	I expect my academic tutors to . . .
1. . . . expect to be told what I should do and how I should do it. 2. . . . want to make choices. 3. . . . want to have lots of opportunities to talk with my peers to consolidate and challenge my ideas. 4. . . . want to do the bare minimum to pass 5. . . . need the readings to be there for me to read. It is a waste of time looking for that sort of thing myself.	1. . . . suggest which journals might be a good starting point. 2. . . . have an open door policy so I can go in any time and ask them how to do something. 3. . . . tell me how many references to include in my bibliography. 4. . . . give me the freedom to be creative in the way I express my ideas. 5. . . . place me in the ideal teaching experience so the best teachers can show me what to do.

Table 2.1: Trainees' course expectations

Now look at Table 2.2. Which statements did you find yourself most akin to? Do they lead you to be more reflective or less reflective?

More reflective statements	Less reflective statements
As a student on an academic course I... 2. ...want to make choices. 3. ...want to have lots of opportunities to talk with my peers to consolidate and challenge my ideas. *I expect my academic tutors to ...* 1. ...suggest which journals might be a good starting point. 4. ...give me the freedom to be creative in the way I express my ideas.	*As a student on an academic course I...* 1. ...expect to be told what I should do and how I should do it. 4. ...want to do the bare minimum to pass. 5. ...need the readings to be there for me to read. It is a waste of time looking for that sort of thing myself. *I expect my academic tutors to ...* 2. ...have an open door policy so I can go in any time and ask them how to do something. 3. ...tell me how many references to include in my bibliography. 5. ...place me in the ideal teaching experience so the best teachers can show me what to do.

Table 2.2: More and less reflective statements

Some of the statements in the activity above were used to encourage you to think about your expectations. There may be some statements you feel are an entitlement for all trainees, not just your own personal expectation. Asking your tutor how to do something, or expecting to be shown what to do on a placement, show a very narrow, limited perspective of learning in higher education and understanding of what teaching is about. However, I have met a surprising number of trainees who believe that these are an entitlement. If you selected a number of statements in the 'less reflective' section of Table 2.2, and this surprises you, reconsider the use of language in the statements such as 'ask how to do something' and 'show me what to do'. In the next chapter Adrian Copping discusses further the opportunities tutorials and placement experiences can create for you to be reflective during your course.

Informal reflection as a valid method of learning

This book is dedicated to helping you improve your own learning and teaching, and helping the children you teach to become more reflective learners themselves. Following some of the guidance will require dedicated time. Other guidance, such as this section and Chapter 4 by Nick Clough, looking at using children's voice as a tool for reflection, suggests that reflection is something that can happen as an integral part of your everyday work.

Research focus

Mason and Johnston-Wilder (2006, p.94) cite a list that their colleague at the Open University, Hilary Evens, drew up after listening to her degree-level students talking about changes in their understanding about their mathematics coursework. Although the context for the original research was mathematics, I suggest that the content of the list works beyond degree-level mathematics and may resonate with your own experience of your academic study.

> *read, recall, recap, recognise, recollect, reconstruct, record, redo, re-express, refer (back), reflect, reformulate, refresh, register, regurgitate, rehearse, reinforce, relate, relearn, remember, remind, reproduce, reread, result, retain, review, revise, revisit, rewrite*

In sharing the list, Mason and Johnston-Wilder are demonstrating that reflection is an active undertaking that encompasses many strategies and that contrary to popular belief learning does not simply happen. Instead, they argue that the act of reflecting is multi-faceted. They explain how 'the prefix re- in reflection implies looking back, but a number of the words in this list do not involve looking back; some represent actions that are performed when doing a task'.

All the actions that Mason and Johnston-Wilder list are strategies that are undertaken actively. They suggest that a learner often reflects informally and that this process 'goes on naturally...without prompting...spontaneously' (Mason and Johnston-Wilder, 2006, p.94). They also explain that informal reflection is key to much learning and that informal reflection is more likely to happen in classrooms where the ethos encourages learners to reflect, make choices, use their initiative and make sense of learning themselves.

Activity

Think about a time when you were trying to improve your knowledge and understanding of a particular aspect of your teacher training. The following list may provide help for you to select one.

- Preparing for an English or mathematics subject knowledge audit
- Planning a lesson for a topic or subject you had not previously taught
- Writing an assessed piece in a style new to you (e.g. a research article or a poster presentation)
- Reworking a conclusion for an essay
- Improving your own subject knowledge for a school history topic or similar
- Identifying and locating possible venues for a class trip

Once you have made your choice, refer to the list in the research focus above. Which strategies were you using? Which of these were an intentional (explicit, planned reflection) undertaking and which were more spontaneous or implicit components of your work? Repeat for another situation.

Are there any strategies on the list that you used in both situations? Are there any that you do not use, or avoid using? Why might that be? Have you identified any strategies that you often default to? Why might that be? How can this work to your advantage and are there any potential dangers in what you have thought about?

The reflection strategies that Mason and Johnston-Wilder have discussed are no doubt the sorts of informal and intuitive strategies that you use every day in your own professional development. The next section looks at a more formal, non-assessed reflection that Schön (1983) would refer to as *reflection on action* (see Introduction for more discussion on Schön).

Non-assessed reflection as a valid method of learning

In the case study below you will meet a trainee called Janet. Her course requires her to regularly submit a piece of 'reflective prose' of not more than 400 words that reflects on her progress against the Teachers' Standards (DfE, 2011). The case study gives a commentary from Janet about how she reworked her assignment before submitting it and provides an insight into her writing process.

Activity
As you read Janet's commentary and scrutinise her work, think about how she:
- uses this reflective assignment to improve her teaching;
- improves her writing;
- understands the value of this sort of reflective process as part of her course.

Case Study: Janet reworks her assignment

I found the first Reflective Prose difficult to complete. I didn't know what to expect and I knew how hard it was to get on the course so I didn't want to show myself up. But after the first one was handed back I felt a lot better. Jason, my tutor, not only used it as the basis of a one-to-one tutorial discussion later on, he also gave me really useful written feedback about how to make my writing more academically appropriate. In my first piece I had a bit of a moment where I went 'blah, blah, blah' and it didn't have as much substance as I'd needed.

$\rightarrow$

I have chosen to share with you my second piece (see Figure 2.2). I started it the same way at first. But I thought it was important to get my ideas out of my head and on the paper as a starting point. It was quite an emotional lesson for me because I really felt I'd let the boys down and although they were unaware of my lack of knowledge, I couldn't challenge them anywhere near how I should have been. Anyway, once I got it on the screen I left it for a couple of days. I find that helps me to distance myself from the emotion of it. Then I printed it out and I went back over it and made loads of changes. You know, I pretend I'm my own tutor, looking at my work! It works best when I have left the work for a few days. Sometimes I'm shocked at how bad it is and other times how insightful I was. I guess it depends what mood I'm in when I write it.

Reflective Prose

Teachers' Standard: 5. Adapt teaching to respond to the strengths and needs of all pupils

For this reflective prose piece I have decided to focus on Standard 5 which is about adapting my teaching to respond to the strengths and needs of all pupils. I have been thinking about a lesson I taught on my serial placement where I had planned a science lesson about (see Appendix 1). Because of my poor science knowledge batteries and I think that my own subject knowledge let me down a bit. I was panicking a lot self confidence in my worried apprehensive before the lesson about any questions that the children might as because I wasn't sure I ask. could answer anything beyond what was on my lesson plan. I had a good way of explaining to them why it was called a battery - because they are made up of a group of cells in a (reference Peacock ...) battery, like a hen battery or a gun battery, I'd heard them talking about gun batteries at children playtime and we had talked about free range eggs because we used the cartons in D&T.

New paragraph. had good knowledge and understanding Sure enough Kevin and Ashmal and George already knew loads about batteries and they During the lesson it became evident that because explained how they had made a battery with zinc and copper at Ashmal's place. They were also knew previously that that talking about how power is the rate at which energy is transferred and how it is measured in They knew energy watts, and how it is calculated by some technical equation. It was all over my head before using ----- at that point that but then they also talked about joules and kilojoules and I actually just left them to it and worked with a group I knew wouldn't ask me any hard questions. I feel like I failed those boys and me by doing that. myself in that lesson.

Figure 2.2: Janet's Reflective Prose

→

For this piece I'd rambled at the beginning and I decided that wasn't needed so I removed it. We'd also been shown how to use appendices to avoid unnecessary description so I put the lesson plan in that way. Jason had also picked me up on not using the correct referencing so I improved that from the last one. On rereading it, I thought 'gee, I had a really downer on myself', so I changed it to be less emotional and more objective. I found that really good because it helped me to focus on what I could change rather than just thinking I couldn't be a teacher because the Standard was unattainable. The class teacher was great. She gave me lots of ideas for strategies to use before, during and after the lesson to support the boys. I was able to reflect on those and decide which one to use later on in the piece.

Like I say, I didn't really get what the point of this writing was all about but now I look forward to them. I can see my progress and how I'm beginning to meet the Standards. At first I was annoyed that they weren't assessed because there is a lot of time spent doing them properly but I'm pleased they aren't because I feel I can be more honest and know that no one is judging me.

It is clear from this case study that Janet values this type of non-assessed reflective work. Not only does she use it to help her to think about her general progress against the Standards towards becoming a teacher, it also forms the basis for a tutorial with her tutor (see Adrian Copping's chapter that follows for more on the value of tutorials). Furthermore, Janet sees the assignment as providing an opportunity to deeply analyse a particular 'critical incident' and think about how she can improve her pedagogical subject knowledge in order to become a better teacher. In doing so, she has made a link between the importance of reading literature about learning and teaching science and its application in the classroom setting. Janet plans space between writing and rereading in order to help her to improve the clarity in her writing and reflection. She acknowledges that she is often emotional when things go well or badly and this process of writing and reflecting also enables her to be more objective. The role of emotion within reflection is discussed in the introduction. There is more about reflective journals in Helen Davenport's chapter.

Formal, assessed reflection as a method of learning: action research

Up until this point the chapter has looked at a number of less formal, non-assessed methods of reflective learning. However, Gibbs (1988, p.9) argues that :

It is not sufficient simply to have an experience in order to learn. Without reflecting upon this experience it may quickly be forgotten, or its learning potential lost. It is from the feelings and thoughts emerging from this reflection that generalisations or concepts can be generated. And it is generalisations that allow new situations to be tackled effectively.

This final section looks at action research as a systematic method of reflective learning. This type of assessed work allows you the time and depth of study required to be able to form generalisations beyond the effect that those reflections discussed to date normally enable.

Action research models

When I talk with trainees and teachers about the role of the reflective practitioner, we discuss the 'plan, do, review' cycle (see Figure 2.3). This cycle can be seen within many aspects of your professional work (Hansen and Vaukins, 2011). For example, you will apply this cycle to plan, teach and evaluate a lesson. Another aspect of your course in which you will see this cycle is action research. In the Introduction you may have read about Dewey's five thinking states. Although there are a number of interpretations of action research methodology (Kemmis, 1997), have you noticed how Dewey's five thinking states tend to be mirrored in basic action research methodology?

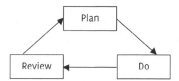

Figure 2.3: The 'plan, do, review' cycle

Cohen, Manion and Morrison (2000, p.235–7) also identify a 'plan, do, review' process within action research but provide a more detailed, eight-stage process:

1. Identification of a problem statement
2. Preliminary discussions between key stake holders
3. Review of literature
4. Modification (if necessary) of problem statement
5. Agreeing on the method
6. Agreeing on evaluation processes
7. Project implementation
8. Analysis and findings of data

Although Cohen et al (2000, p.237) stress that this is only a *basic framework*, it gives Stage 8 as an end point. This was also a criticism of Dewey's five thinking stages (see Introduction), but depending on the type of reflective research or assignment you are undertaking, this linear process might be all you need.

However, Hansen and Vaukins (2011) discussed how analysis of data often leads to more questions than you started with! Therefore, you could be interested in a longer, cyclical process, which is often identified as fundamental to action research (see, for example, Hitchcock and Hughes, 1995). Zuber-Skerritt (1996) reviewed a number of action research methodologies and identified that many of them involved a cyclical process: (1) strategic planning; (2) implementation; (3) observation, evaluation and self-evaluation; and (4) critical and self-critical evaluation on parts 1–3, to inform and make decisions for the next cycle. Each time the process of decision-making is entered into, it consolidates prior knowledge and clarifies what steps are to be taken next. Another model to represent action research is offered by Kemmis and McTaggart (1981, p.2) who refer to a spiral in their action research work: 'and the spiral of action, monitoring, evaluation and replanning continues'.

Emotion and personal judgement in assessed pieces

Some trainees are concerned that they do not feel able to be honest in their assignments when they are assessed items. If you share this concern, you should discuss it with your tutor. Additionally, it is important to remember that assessed assignments involving any type of action research require systematic reflection that brings together theory and practice. As discussed in the Introduction and in Janet's case study above, emotions and concerns about professional standing exist, and remain evident even during more formal methods of reflection. Strauss and Corbin (1998, p.97) explain that it is not possible to be bias-free, but 'the important thing is to recognise when either our own or the respondents' biases, assumptions, or beliefs are intruding into the analysis ... we must be able to stand back and examine the data at least somewhat objectively'. Additionally, qualitative research of this type maintains a high validity through the 'honesty, depth, richness and scope of the data achieved' (Cohen et al, 2000, p.105). This can only be a positive aspect of this more formal approach to reflective learning as a teacher and trainee teacher.

Activity
At the beginning of this chapter you were asked to note down your genuine thoughts, feelings and ideas about 'reflective practice'. Now return to those notes. How has your thinking shifted? Make notes to record the shift. Now consider what actions you need to carry out in order to demonstrate how your thinking has shifted. You may wish to develop an action plan that responds to the following questions. What are your goals or next steps? How are you going to achieve the steps? What milestones will you expect to see on the way? Who/what will help you to achieve your goals? How will you know when you have achieved them? What impact do you envisage achieving your goals will have on your teaching and academic work? How will you celebrate your achievements?

Learning Outcomes Review

In this chapter you will have developed your understanding of how 'reflective practice' can have a significant number of positive effects on your learning. These included purposes such as learning from experience, supporting professional and academic understanding, developing critical thinking, enhancing ownership of learning, developing evaluative skills, enhancing problem-solving skills, providing self-empowerment, supporting behaviour and feelings, enhancing creativity, improving writing, improving communication, and enhancing interaction with others. All of these purposes of reflection lead to improvement in your teaching and your academic work, be it informal, formal, non-assessed or assessed.

Self-assessment questions

1. What are the main purposes you use reflection for?
2. Identify at least one aspect in your current study where you use:
   a. informal, intuitive reflection;
   b. non-assessed reflections for another audience;
   c. reflection in assessed pieces of academic work.
3. If you haven't yet done so, visit the first and final activities of this chapter. Use some of the prompts and suggestions in Mike Pezet's coaching chapter, Chapter 5, to take your action planning further.

Further reading

Ghaye, T. (2011) *Teaching and Learning Through Reflective Practice: A Practical Guide for Positive Action*, 2nd ed. London: Routledge.
This new edition looks at how reflection can positively transform your teaching. It provides six key ideas on which reflective practice is developed and focuses on drawing out the type of teacher you want to be and developing your strengths.

Hansen, A. and Vaukins, D. (2011) *Mathematics Across the Primary Curriculum*. Exeter: Learning Matters.
Chapter 8 looks at researching teaching and learning and offers an additional model for action research that includes reflection through a process that includes systematic review.

Pollard, A. (2008) *Reflective Teaching: Evidence-informed Professional Practice*, 3rd ed. London: Continuum International.
A well-established and comprehensive textbook, with accompanying website (www.rtweb.info) for trainees and teachers on all professional development journeys, developed by an editorial team chaired by Andrew Pollard. Andrew Pollard was the director of TLRP, who published the ten evidence-informed pedagogic principles you met in the Introduction to this book.

References

Beaty, L. (1997) *Developing Your Teaching Through Reflective Practice*. Birmingham: SEDA.

Boud, D. (1995) *Enhancing Learning Through Self Assessment*. London: Kogan Page.

Claxton, G. (1999) *Wise Up: The Challenge of Lifelong Learning*. London: Bloomsbury.

Cohen, L., Manion, L. and Morrison, K. (2000) *Research Methods in Education. 5th ed.* London: RoutledgeFalmer.

Conway, N. and Briner, R.B. (2005) *Understanding Psychological Contracts at Work: A Critical Evaluation of Theory and Research.* Oxford: Oxford University Press.

Cullinane, N. and Dundon, T. (2006) The psychological contract: a critical review. *International Journal of Management Reviews*, 8(2): 113–29.

Department for Education (2011) *Teachers' Standards.* London: DfE. Reference: DFE-00066-2011.

Gibbs, G. (1988) *Learning by Doing: A Guide to Teaching and Learning Methods.* Oxford: Further Education Unit.

Hansen, A. and Vaukins, D. (2011) *Mathematics Across the Primary Curriculum.* Exeter: Learning Matters.

Hitchcock, G. and Hughes, D. (1995) *Research and the Teacher: A Qualitative Introduction to School-based Research.* 2nd ed. London: Routledge.

International Transactional Analysis Association (2011) *About TA.* Available at: http://itaaworld.org/index.php/about-ta (accessed 23/11/11).

Kemmis, S. (1997) Action research. In J.P. Keeves (ed) *Educational Research, Methodology, and Measurement: An International Handbook*, 2nd ed. Oxford: Elsevier Science.

Kemmis, S. and McTaggart, R. (eds) (1981) *The Action Research Planner.* Geelong, Victoria: Deakin University Press.

Mason, J. and Johnston-Wilder, S. (2006) *Designing and Using Mathematical Tasks.* St Albans: Tarquin Publications.

McGill, I. and Brockbank, A. (1998) *Facilitating Reflective Learning in Higher Education.* Buckingham: Open University.

Moon, J. (1999) *Learning Journals: A Handbook for Academics, Students and Professional Development.* London: Kogan Page.

Schön, D.A. (1983) *The Reflective Practitioner: How Professionals Think in Action.* London: Temple Smith.

Strauss, A. and Corbin, J. (1998) *Basics of Qualitative Research: Techniques and Procedures for Developing Grounded Theory*, 2nd ed. London: SAGE Publications.

Zuber-Skerritt, O. (1996) Emancipatory action research for organisational change and management development. In O. Zuber-Skerritt (ed) *New Directions in Action Research.* London: Falmer.

3. Reflective learning and teaching opportunities
Adrian Copping

Learning Outcomes	

By the end of this chapter you will:
- understand the importance of linking theoretical perspectives with practical experience to facilitate a greater depth of reflection;
- understand the variety of ways that reflection on and in action can occur and how they can be managed to maximise learning and development;
- challenge the assumptions that you bring to and have about learning and teaching.

Introduction

In the previous chapter you read how reflective learning is an essential component of becoming a teacher and continuing your professional development throughout your career. In this chapter, you will explore how experiences, both in and out of the classroom, provide significant opportunities for reflection and learning. The chapters that follow suggest strategies and methods for making the most of these opportunities in more detail.

> *Reflective Practice is a label, used by some, that refers to the use of different methods which, arguably, offer the possibility of helping us make sense of the different encounters that we have with others in particular social contexts.*

> (Ghaye, 2011, p.35)

In this definition Ghaye makes two very interesting suggestions, which were reflected in the Introduction. The first suggests that there are methods of reflection to use and second, there is a social aspect to it: different encounters with others in social contexts. Ghaye goes on to argue that reflection is much more than a method and uses the phrase 'reflective learning' (2011, p.35) as a more palatable term. This term takes away the connotation of a method to get to a 'right' answer and puts in its place something more inclusive.

Identifying opportunities for reflective learning

So, let's begin a typical trainee teacher's learning journey and consider some of the reflection opportunities offered that contribute to your becoming a confident and competent qualified teacher.

Prior to your course: studying assumptions

Brookfield (1995) puts forward the idea that reflection is *hunting assumptions* (1995, p.2). What assumptions about teaching, education and yourself are you bringing to the course? These assumptions will come from your past experiences of education and will usually involve some situations that you found yourself in as a learner that you are not anxious to put others through. Perhaps it is experiences like these that have led to you making the decision to want to be a teacher.

Research Focus

In order to aid the assumption hunt, Brookfield suggests three broad categories of assumptions which are useful to consider. The first is 'paradigmatic assumptions' (1995, p.2). It is these assumptions we hold that shape our world and order our thinking and understanding about it. For example, do you hold the assumption that children will learn given the right environment within which to do so? Challenging these world-shaping assumptions can be incredibly uncomfortable as they are crucial to who we are as people. The second is 'prescriptive assumptions' (1995, p.3). These assumptions tend to be an effect of what our paradigmatic assumptions are. For example, if you believe that children will learn if the environment is right then you would assume and take it for granted that the teacher would put creating the best possible learning environment for their children at the top of their agenda. The third, 'causal assumptions' (1995, p.3) is all to do with how we assume the world works in terms of how events are caused and what the effect is. For example, if we show children that we make mistakes then the effect is that it creates trust in the classroom and creates an ethos of 'it's OK to make mistakes'. Similarly, we may assume that if we provide children with marking criteria to improve their writing it will mean that they then can take control over improving their writing to attain a higher grade.

Why is understanding your own assumptions important?

If you understand what your own assumptions about teaching and learning are then you are in a prime position to start challenging them and begin to start seeing events and ideas from other viewpoints. Brookfield states: 'Central to the reflective process is this attempt to see things from a variety of viewpoints. Reflective teachers seek to probe beneath the veneer of a commonsense reading of experience' (1995, p.7).

You will come to the start of your course with a variety of prior experiences. You may have had other employment in schools, such as teaching assistant, learning mentor or sports coach. Your experience has shaped your assumptions and has started already to impact on the type of teacher you will be.

Case Study: Challenging assumptions

Ian came to his teacher education course having spent all his experience working in primary schools with children from low socio-economic backgrounds. Ian is a very caring, generous young man with a passion to see children succeed and feel good about themselves. However, Ian had seen a lack of attainment from many of the children he had worked with and formed a link between a lack of support at home, a lack of aspiration from the children, poor socio-economic background and a lack of attainment. Ian came to his studies with this experience.

On his first placement Ian was placed in a Year 6 class, again in a school with children predominantly from a low socio-economic background. Ian's first lesson was pitched very low, based on his expectations, and he was shocked when he found that the class had finished the work within ten minutes. The majority of Ian's class were bright and attaining highly. This shook Ian's assumptions very strongly.

What type of teacher do you want to be?

Is this something you have begun to consider? Have you pictured yourself commanding a class of 30 11-year-olds, hanging on your every word as you expound some concepts with skill and clarity? Have you pictured yourself in among 30 five-year-olds, playing with them, facilitating their exploration of the world with carefully planned activities linked to a central theme? Have you pictured something else? Are these the assumptions you have about how it will be – if I do this then this will happen? Are you sure? The main question that needs to be asked at this point is this: Are you ready to start the reflective process by challenging these visions and perhaps therefore challenging deeply held assumptions about teachers, teaching and learning?

Module and programme design

One of the most significant opportunities to reflect on learning through centre-based work is to take the opportunities offered through the design of modules that you are studying. Taking the idea that learning occurs in both centre-based contexts and during placements, there will be opportunities to make links between them both.

Case Study: Reflection as a continuing process

Helen, a trainee teacher, took part in a behaviour management morning with the whole cohort of students and their tutors. Helen worked in a group of 12 students where they had to role-play different behaviour management scenarios. Each student took a turn as the teacher and each as a child displaying certain types of behaviour. Helen found some of the techniques she was taught particularly useful. During her reflections, Helen felt more confident with a small range of techniques and felt they might work.

$\rightarrow$

> During her first week on placement, Helen had the opportunity to enact some of these techniques with her Year 3 class. Although they did not work particularly well, during her evaluation meeting with her class teacher at the end of the day, Helen discussed refining the techniques for the class, the children, and that an approach and its success was often dependent on the relationship the teacher had with the class.

While reflection is clearly occurring in this example, there is a sense that reflecting on behaviour management could stop here and the opportunities offered during your modules has not been fully taken up. Reflection should be a continual process. Ward and McCotter (2004) map this out in a reflection rubric, stating that reflection should lead to a fundamental transformation in conceptualising ideas. However, if reflection is truly a process then their rubric should be visited and revisited, or reconceptualised as a cycle. This being the case then, the concept, in this example behaviour management, should be visited, revisited, challenged and re-evaluated as new experiences are brought to bear on it.

Activity

Where are these opportunities? One question to ask is: What is happening in my centre-based work before and after placement? Is there opportunity for me to share my learning? Are sessions available for me to spend time with my peers and tutor making sense of my learning experiences?

Making sense of learning experiences can be a difficult and problematic process. Ghaye and Ghaye (1998) suggest that 'central to this process is our ability to reflect constructively and critically on our teaching intentions, the ends we have in mind and the means we might use to achieve them' (p.19). They go on to suggest that reflective conversations can be effective in supporting this process.

Reflective conversations

What makes a reflective conversation? A reflective conversation should not just be a description of events directed towards a sympathetic or even empathetic ear. Ghaye and Ghaye (1998) suggest that it should focus on values – the educational values that make us who we are as teachers and guide what we do. By definition, a reflective conversation should involve an element of challenge, challenging the actions taken in a given situation and perhaps even the values upon which they are based.

Research Focus

Ghaye (2011) gives ten principles that characterise the practice of reflection. These are:

1. Having a shared discourse about what reflective practice is.

2. The fact that it is energised and developed through experience.

3. It is a process that involves a 'turn' from looking at the critical incident to also ourselves and significant others.

4. Reflective practice is about learning to account for ourselves.

5. It is about enquiry, not just collecting data or evidence.

6. It is about knowledge-creation and interest-serving.

7. It is enacted by those who are critical thinkers.

8. Reflective practice is a way of decoding a symbolic landscape.

9. It is the interface between notions of theory and practice.

10. It is at the centre of how we learn and know.

Ghaye also gives a detailed exploration of reflective conversations, including examples. Types of questions to use are suggested and the effects on learning are discussed through a very clear annotated example. Some of the fundamental questions Ghaye suggests are as follows.

What is my teaching like? What is successful in my teaching? How do I know this? Why is it like this? How has it come to be this way? What are the effects of my teaching on those I am working with? What do I need to change to improve what I do? How might I do this?

Having opportunities to reflect and make links between centre and placement based learning is crucial to your development as a reflective and effective practitioner.

Activity
Select a module you are currently undertaking. How has the module been designed to support your own reflective learning?

Centre-based learning: bridging the theory/practice gap

Everything you undertake during your course of study will enable you to become a more confident and competent teacher. All the modules you undertake, the seminars and lectures you engage with, have one purpose: to equip you to become an effective teacher, one who understands how children learn and is able to meet their needs so that they can attain, develop and flourish under your command. But you have some work to do: you have to bridge the gap between the centre-based activity and the placement learning by making sense of it and applying it. Take a questioning stance to all you do both in school and out.

Research Focus

Brookfield (1995) suggests that a number of changes occur in your thinking and understanding. These changes are crucial to your development as a reflective teacher. The changes below are identified by Brookfield but the application of them to beginning teachers is my own. First, Brookfield suggests that as we become more critically reflective we begin to see that our teaching is directly aligned to what we believe about teaching and learning. The curriculum we teach and the recommended approaches are there to be reframed within our particular context. As a beginning teacher it may be starting to consider why you are teaching with particular resources or particular elements of a topic when it is perhaps not meeting the needs of the learners. It may be about considering why the classroom tables are organised in groups and clusters. When we start to reflect critically, we start to ask the question 'why?' and are opening our minds to the idea that things do not always have to be fixed and static but can be fluid and reframed according to the context and learners' needs.

What assumptions do you hold about the type of teacher you will be once you have completed your course of study? Perhaps you assume that you will be the finished article? Brookfield (1995) suggests that as we move along the reflective process we see ourselves as continuously evolving professionals. As a beginning teacher you should see yourself evolving as you reflect on your seminars and lectures, bringing them to your practice and as you move from your practice into your lectures and seminars.

Activity

How can you apply the learning you are engaging in at the centre? What does it mean for you? What have you learned in each seminar that you can take forward and become a better teacher as a result?

Spend ten minutes at the end of a seminar asking yourself, what two or three key points will you take away from it that will help you become a more effective teacher?

Reflection in action: making connections

As a result of joining up our experiences, our teaching becomes what Brookfield terms 'a connective activity' (1995, p.42). Schön would probably term this *reflection in action* (see Introduction for more about reflection in action). If you have a critical stance to your teaching then your teaching will become more of an art than a technical set of competencies. As you respond to and connect with your learners, and connect with the curriculum and the ideologies that underpin your teaching, your teaching becomes responsive, often more experimental and you will take risks (see Figure 3.1).

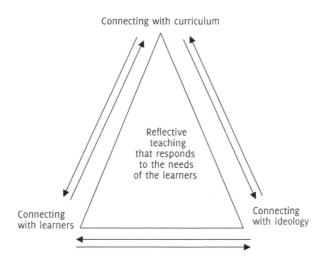

Connecting with curriculum

Reflective teaching that responds to the needs of the learners

Connecting with learners

Connecting with ideology

Figure 3.1: Reflection connections

Taking risks can be deemed dangerous by a beginning teacher: because of your huge desire, personally, professionally and often financially, to pass the course, you will not wish to jeopardise your chances by trying something a little different in the classroom. However, what we are talking about should be at the heart of your teaching: that desire to meet the needs of the learners in your care. This often requires getting past the 'technical rationality' (Schon, 1996, p.12) and view of teaching as a set of technical competencies because what happens when the situation or context you are in demands something else? Schön states that 'reflection in action . . . is central to the art through which practitioners sometimes cope with the troublesome "divergent" situations of practice' (1996, p.27).

As you reflect in action and on action you create a classroom that is less about you as the teacher and more about us all as a community of learners in the classroom. We realise that the children need to be active participants in learning and work with us to create meaningful learning experiences.

Finally, Brookfield (1995) suggests that as we reflect we find our voice as professionals. Your learning, both at the centre and on placement, helps create the teachers you are and puts some flesh on the bones of the type of teacher you want to be. As you find your voice, your assumptions may be challenged, and as you reflect on the seminars, the ideas, beliefs, thoughts, philosophical positions and activities that are presented to you, you form your own ideas, opinions and ideals that may well be refined, challenged or supported through practice and experience.

Reflecting on your subject knowledge

In any course of study you bring curriculum subject knowledge with you. It is important to recognise this, as when embarking on something new it is easy to forget your existing knowledge and how you can apply it to a new situation. You may need to challenge your assumptions here. You may assume that you have enough knowledge in order to teach in the primary school. This is a dangerous assumption to make. As you get to know the primary curriculum better, and as you work with more and a variety of children you will begin to realise that both what you are required to teach and who you are required to teach are highly demanding. You may also find that the pedagogical understanding you need demands a higher level of subject knowledge than you discover you have.

Auditing subject knowledge

Auditing your subject knowledge prior to starting the course, at the beginning, and then keeping track of your progress, is crucial to your success as a teacher. It may be helpful for you to start with the core subjects of English, mathematics and science. Your provider may well expect you to carry out an audit before starting the course. There are other tools, prior to beginning your course of study, that will enable you to audit your knowledge and perhaps allow you to discover what you do not know.

It is important to track your own understanding and progress throughout curriculum study during the course. Table 3.1 is an example of a tool that may help you to reflect on your development in this area. It may help identify gaps and areas to develop as well as chart any action that you need to take. Some subject associations websites also provide online subject knowledge audits for you to work through.

Curriculum English Module				
Session title	Subject knowledge covered (broad)	Areas to develop (specific)	Action	Revisit date
What makes a good English lesson	Role of talk in learning, scaffolding			
Shared and guided reading	Principles and processes of teaching reading			
Shared and guided writing	Principles and processes of teaching writing			
Practical phonics	Synthetic phonics Alphabetic code			

Table 3.1: An example of an audit tool to support reflection and action needed as subject knowledge develops through centre-based seminars

Activity

Using Table 3.1 as a template, reflect on each of your curriculum subject sessions or curriculum subject input you have at your training centre base. Note down the specific areas that you need to develop arising from the sessions and seek support in setting some specific actions to develop them. Make sure you have identified when you will revisit these areas to check your understanding and application. As a result you may find there are other areas identified as needing to be developed!

Utilising peer support to aid reflection

Reflection-on-action tends to be a solitary activity. After an event or lesson you may note down reflections on your performance and on the children's ability to meet the learning outcomes. You may reflect on the pace of the lesson, on the resources used and on the success of the activities. However, as Brookfield (1995) states, 'Critical reflection is an irreducibly social process. It happens best when we enlist colleagues to help us see our practice in new ways' (1995, p.141). The importance of working with colleagues should not be underestimated, as Mike Pezet shows in his chapter on coaching, and Pete Dudley and Elizabeth Gowing demonstrate in their chapter exploring the power of Lesson Study.

Our own perceptions of what occurred in an event may not always be a true reflection. Our own bias, and our own beliefs about our prowess as teachers can skew the way we see particular events. When we share our experiences of teaching with our peers and they reflect back to us their perceptions we can often see new insights, or certainly view the event in a different way. These perceptions can help us locate the aspects of our practice that need more work. However, these types of conversations can only really be effective under certain conditions. With reference to reflective conversations, discussed earlier in the chapter, and considering critical conversations, Brookfield (1995) states that 'it requires a moral and political culture characterized by an openness to diverse perspectives and ideologies, and a respectful acknowledgement of the importance of each person's contribution' (1995, p.140).

Critical conversations do not just occur when beginning teachers sit together and start sharing their experiences. There is a need for preparation and training in order to ensure that this reflective opportunity moves from a sharing, caring session to one where perceptions are challenged, changed and discussed. The express goal of this is to help you become the best teacher you can be. To generate these types of conversations, agreed ground rules need to evolve. An assumption we may have is that students on a professional course will be the types of students who will know how to talk to each other with respect and without one-upmanship. It is important that a dialogic relationship is established between all members of the group so that the conversation does not shut down.

Utilising technology

Peer support may not be face to face. Many ITT courses expect student teachers to use virtual learning environments to reflect upon and discuss key issues. This is discussed in more detail by Helen Davenport in Chapter 8.

Many ITT courses are developed around e-portfolios, in which student teachers are expected to reflect upon and track their development throughout their course. This is shared with their tutors and becomes a discussion tool during tutorials. These portfolios may form the basis of assessments. Crucially, the purpose is that all the trainee's development and reflection throughout placements and academic work are drawn together in one place.

Research focus

Brookfield (1995) follows the process of critical conversation, from creating ground rules to different approaches to the conversation itself. Brookfield discusses various frameworks for effective critical conversation, so that you as a beginning teacher can begin to make more informed choices about your work.

A key element Brookfield emphasises here is using a critical incident to begin the conversation. Once ground rules have been set, a member of the group recounts an incident (perhaps from placement), a general theme can emerge and this can set the agenda for the discussion. As people contribute and themes emerge then members realise that they share similar issues; what they thought were often idiosyncratic failings or inadequacies in their own practice are actually common experiences. This provides great encouragement for the group. Brookfield states that high points should also be shared. Critical reflection can sometimes lead to a crisis of despair, so there is also a need for critical conversations to celebrate victories.

Personal/academic tutorials

It is very important for you to establish these ground rules for critical and reflective conversations with your personal tutor. In the above case study about Helen, the role of the personal tutor is crucial to the effectiveness of reflection. The module is punctuated by tutorials to provide several pit stops over its duration and also the duration of the course. As a result, your personal tutor may well be the member of the centre-based staff team who works with you on the most regular basis. This is an opportunity you need to utilise.

In order for the personal tutorial to be effective there are a number of things that need to be in place. Demarest et al (2004), cited in Ghaye (2011), developed the Mobius Model. The six qualities of this model are represented in Table 3.2.

Mutual understanding	Each person feels understood and understands the other. This is not the same as agreeing with each other.
Possibility	All parties recognise something new that is desirable and realistic to create.
Commitment	There is agreement to priorities among goals and values that will direct action.
Capability	This exists when everyone agrees a way to fulfil the commitments
Responsibility	Everyone agrees who will carry out the commitments.
Acknowledgement	There is mutual recognition of what has been accomplished and what is still missing for the commitments to be fully realised.

Table 3.2: The Mobius Model (adapted from Ghaye, 2011, p.48)

This model puts forward a clear process for a reflective and/or critical conversation in the context of a personal tutorial. There is a sense of mutuality here, where the reflection is being facilitated and the outcomes are sought together with the facilitator through what Ghaye calls a 'strengths-based conversational process'(2011, p.48).

You need to come prepared for the tutorial. Make sure you have done any reading and have an agenda. While your personal tutor may also have an agenda, you need to prepare something to reflect on and something to have a critical conversation about. For example, if you are asked to come to the tutorial having considered some personal targets for placement, make sure you do that, and also bring your thought processes with you. Your tutor may well be asking some uncomfortable questions, such as 'Why have you chosen that?', so you also need to come with a sense of openness.

As well as a lack of preparedness, a number of other things can contribute to your tutorial being ineffective. The first is coming thinking you can't change the situation, using language such as 'What's the point?', 'It won't work,' 'I can't do it,' 'What can I do, they're not my class?' The second is not taking responsibility – being passive. For example, you may uncritically accept what you are told; you may write it down but not act upon it. You need to come to these conversations with an open attitude and mind, believing that what you are reflecting upon can be changed and improvement can occur. The challenge is, of course, to continue reflecting when the perceived problem is solved. The goal of reflection is in part about problem-solving but it is also about gaining new insights, and understanding new philosophies and paradigms. Mike Pezet discusses attitude and willingness to change in his chapter about coaching.

Case Study: Leanne and Mark reflect on 1:1 tutorials

Mark is a university tutor and has responsibility for a group of 26 PGCE students. He teaches them for some modules and is heavily involved in helping them prepare for placements as well as supporting them through their course.

$\rightarrow$

Mark states that tutorials are a fantastic opportunity to meet the student on a 1:1 basis, to look at individual progress, targets, their own journey and get to know them as an individual. It also helps him look at how he can help personalise learning for that student.

Leanne, one of Mark's tutor group, shares this view. 'Although Mark teaches us and we get to talk to him a bit, it's not the same as meeting on a 1:1 basis with him. He can get to know our individual struggles and challenges and help us individually with anything we are struggling with. For me having that 1:1 contact is essential because I always come away feeling that I'm on the right track, I'm OK and I know what I'm doing. It's like a pit stop, I suppose.'

Placement-based learning

As a trainee teacher, you may feel that reflection is not very high on your priority list. You are getting to grips with managing the children, managing the classroom, managing the resources and managing the routines, as well as planning and teaching for the first time. Throughout this next section of the chapter I want to suggest that, first, if you want to progress and develop as a teacher then reflection is vital. Second, there are some practical and non-time-consuming approaches to reflection that are more about a change in thought process and attitude than additional work on top of everything else.

Lesson evaluation

Spending a short amount of time on evaluating in the break after each lesson can be incredibly beneficial and save you a multitude of hours, guesswork and form-filling. Lesson evaluations should usually focus on two aspects: your teaching and the children's learning. There is no need to write lengthy prose; if you did this for all your lessons, very little teaching would occur. A key question is, then, how do you know how it went? When I posed this to a small group of trainee teachers towards the end of their one-year Primary PGCE course, they said, 'Because we are told'. This demonstrates that these particular students were not actively involved in their own development and learning.

For you to become an effective practitioner you need to take responsibility for your progress. I'm not suggesting that you shouldn't ask for feedback from experienced teachers, just that you shouldn't wait for them to give it to you. You should be reflecting on what you know to be good practice from your previous experience and centre-based training and make some professional judgements. Many students tend to begin their evaluations with 'It went well.' Medwell (2005) states: 'This is an ineffective evaluation because it tells the reader [or yourself] . . . that the trainee survived to teach again. What went well? Does well mean the children learned something ?' (2005, p.61).

What you need to consider are your placement targets. For example, if you are working on assessment for learning then you need to monitor and make notes regarding this element:

whether it was planned effectively, whether it was manageable. Did your method work? Did you get the information you needed to take further action? There is no need to evaluate everything; focus on your particular target areas. Just make notes; there is no need to type anything up.

The important thing about evaluation is that it leads to action in your planning. Medwell (2005) states that 'The very best planning is the sort that clearly uses evidence from children's previous attainment and leads to influence the planning and teaching of the next session or lesson' (2005, p.61). This is what you are aiming for.

Weekly evaluation

It can be helpful to take time out at the end of a week to reflect on how things have gone in terms of your progression. Again, this evaluation can easily become descriptive and be a paper-pushing exercise only. Gibbs' (1988) reflective cycle is a useful framework to support a deeper level of reflection while reflecting on your practice. Below is my adaptation.

- *Description*: What is the stimulant for reflection (incident, event, theoretical idea)? What are you going to reflect on?
- *Feelings*: What were your reactions and feelings?
- *Evaluation*: What was good and bad about the experience? Make value judgements.
- *Analysis*: What sense can you make of the situation? Bring in ideas from outside the experience to help you. What was really going on?
- *Conclusions (general)*: What can be concluded, in a general sense, from these experiences and the analyses you have undertaken?
- *Conclusions (specific)*: What can be concluded about your own specific, unique, personal situation or ways of working?
- *Personal action plans*: What are you going to do differently in this type of situation next time? What steps are you going to take on the basis of what you have learned?

If you respond to each of these questions in order you will be thinking deeply about events that have occurred. This includes drawing conclusions and identifying future actions, thus making the evaluation useful for your future development.

Assessment of children's work

As you evaluate your lessons you will reflect on the children's attainment and whether they have met the learning outcomes you have identified. This reflection should lead you to a number of questions that will need addressing in order to help you develop. Probable questions are outlined in Figure 3.2.

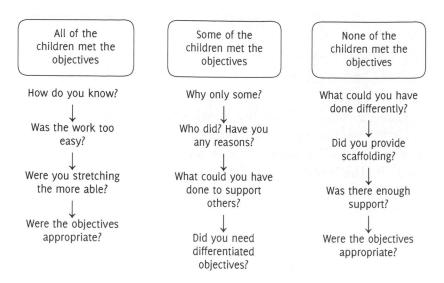

Figure 3.2: Applying assessing children's work to reflecting on teaching

Notice that none of these questions refers to the children but actually to your teaching. Your teaching, which includes your explanations, questioning, behaviour management strategies, the activities, the objectives themselves, the resources, support and outcomes you expect, directly impacts on the children's ability to attain in your lessons. Building on this idea, Nick Clough discusses using children's voice as another reflection strategy in the next chapter.

Using the framework in Figure 3.2 to help you reflect on this will support you in planning the next lesson and in matching your teaching approaches to the needs of your learners.

Activity

When assessing children's work after a lesson, use the questions in Figure 3.2 to evaluate your teaching. Choose the strand most relevant to the lesson you are reflecting on.

Note the information the children's work gives you and note the action that needs to happen as a result.

Include this as part of your lesson evaluation and make sure you have signposted how this has affected your next lesson in your planning file. You could highlight the changes you have made as a result. This is highly effective reflection on action.

Lisa Murtagh's chapter on self- and peer-assessment provides a detailed discussion on the difference between assessment and evaluation, and offers practical suggestions for using assessment yourself and for children. The next section looks at how you can use video for self- and/or peer-evaluation of your teaching.

Self-observation of teaching

Observing yourself teach is a very helpful way of helping you reflect on your own practice. This can be done by setting up a video camera in your classroom and videoing a lesson. Make sure you go through the necessary confidentiality procedures with this: you will need to speak to the headteacher of the school prior to embarking on this and it may well require permission from parents of the children in your class. One of the main benefits of self-observation is that it helps you realise the reality of what is happening in your classroom. When you are teaching, you don't really get a full picture of what is going on.

Activity

Have a go at videoing one of your lessons. Be sure to discuss this with the headteacher and follow the agreed procedures for confidentiality. Agree arrangements for what will happen to the data on the tape once you have finished.

Note down what surprises you. What were your initial reflections after the lesson? How do they compare with what you've seen now that you've watched it back?

In some work I did with some students recently, the recognition of reality was really important. Below is an extract from the discussion group that followed the students videoing their practice (Copping, 2010,p.9):

2: '... the general dynamic of the room. It was very different to how I perceived it ... '
4: '... What did you think it was?'
2: '... I thought there was a lot more noise, a lot more pushing. Watching it back, I mean, they're not that bad'.
(Participants 2 and 4 from 1st iteration of data collection)

What will you take from videoing your teaching? How will it impact on the next lesson you teach or the way you think and feel about your work as a teacher?

In my research (Copping, 2010) I discuss the character and principles of reflection as well as approaches to it. The research consisted of two iterations. Both involved student teachers videoing their practice and then meeting as a focus group afterwards to share their experiences and discuss their findings and reflections. The conclusion to the first iteration raised one key point, concerning reflection used for two purposes: (1) the notion of 'incidental learning', the type of learning that is unplanned and emerges; and (2) the 'reinforcement of learning', where video and self-observation are used to ratify a mentor's comment.

The participants all reported that the videoing of practice had supported their own reflection very effectively. It gave them a sense of the reality of the classroom and helped them to understand that their perspective of events from the front of the class may not always be objective. This research demonstrated that the reflective process continued to a greater depth when an incident unplanned for or previously unnoticed occurred during playback of the teaching. Where student teachers used the video to ratify comments, they stopped reflecting when the perceived problem was 'solved'. The key point here is that reflection should be more of a transformational process and not merely evidence to support decisions made.

The research also raised some important considerations about reflection as a social process. Reflective conversation does not just occur naturally. It needs to be carefully planned, ground rules need to be agreed and parameters set for it to be effective in supporting the reflective process. Putting these in place should facilitate the confidence to share areas for development and honest appraisal without fear of criticism and unsupportive judgement.

What about feedback from my school-based mentor?

Formal feedback

Your formal observations will be a key opportunity for you to reflect on your practice. The feedback you receive from the observation should be discussed with you and this discussion between yourself and the mentor should lead to new actions, approaches and improved ways of doing things. It is important, as discussed before, that you need to come prepared for this and not just passively accept what you are told. This 'assessment' of your teaching is something that should be done *with* you, not *to* you, and therefore you have a responsibility to be involved in the discussion.

Informal feedback

Remember that there are lots of other opportunities to get feedback on your teaching. These informal occasions can be just as valuable. You may choose to do playground duty with your class teacher and have a 'playground conversation'. Take ten minutes prior to a staff meeting and bring your class teacher a cup of coffee, or it could just be a 'corridor conversation'. Use these opportunities to get the information you need. Your time in school with experienced professionals is crucial to your success as a reflective teacher and taking every chance to discuss with them, learn from them and reflect upon the experience is going to help you. Make the most of these valuable informal opportunities.

Learning Outcomes Review

This chapter has considered the opportunities available for you to engage in the process of reflection. Using a learning journey, it went through opportunities pre-course and during centre-based and placement-based learning to understand the importance of reflection. It also discussed the personal and professional benefits of being reflective in your approaches. Practical advice was given on embedding reflection into your practice and gaining the most from your centre-based learning. You have considered the importance of linking theoretical perspectives with practical experience to facilitate a greater depth of reflection. You have been challenged to think about the variety of ways that reflection on and in action can occur and how they can be managed to maximise learning and development. You have been asked to consider and challenge the assumptions that you bring to and have about learning and teaching as you start the course. Through the process of reflection you have been encouraged to notice how these assumptions have changed.

Self-assessment questions

1. As you consider your lesson planning and weekly planning, how is the scaffolding of learning evident within them?
2. How would you develop your skills more effectively if you drew on Gibbs' (1988) model for reflection to evaluate your lessons?
3. What different approaches could you use to reflect on your action? For example, audio recording.
4. What will you do if you notice your teaching approaches are not proving effective? How will you change things? What will you learn from this experience?

Further Reading

Bolton, G. (2010) Reflective Practice: Writing and Professional Development. London. SAGE Publications.
This text is largely about writing reflectively. As well as looking at reflection it discusses reflexivity and provides some helpful tools to support reflective writing in different forms.

Brookfield, S. (1995) *Becoming a Critically Reflective Teacher*. San Francisco: Jossey-Bass. Read Chapter 7, 'Holding critical conversations about teaching', to learn more about professional, dialogic conversations.

Ghaye, T. (2011) *Teaching and Learning through Reflective Practice: A Practical Guide for Positive Action*, 2nd ed. Abingdon: Routledge.
Chapter 3 provides some views of the nature of reflection-on-practice and presents ten principles that characterise the practice of reflection shared in the research focus in this chapter.

Ghaye, A. and Ghaye, K. (1998) *Teaching and Learning through Critical Reflective Practice.* London: David Fulton
This text advocates a strengths-based reflective practice approach that is very positive and supportive. The text is practical but also gets the reader to think beyond events to being reflective about values as well.

Hayes, D. (2011) Establishing your own teacher identity. In A. Hansen (ed) *Primary Professional Studies.* Exeter: Learning Matters.
This chapter will encourage you to think further about what type of teacher you would like to be.

Challen, D. (2007) *Primary English: Audit and Test.* Exeter: Learning Matters.

Mooney, C. and Fletcher, M. (2007) *Primary Mathematics: Audit and Test*. Exeter: Learning Matters.

Sharpe, J. and Byrne, J. (2007) *Primary Science: Audit and test*. Exeter: Learning Matters.

These will support your subject knowledge.

References

Brookfield, S. (1995) *Becoming a Critically Reflective Teacher*. San Francisco: Jossey Bass.

Challen, D. (2007) *Primary English: Audit and Test*, 3rd ed. Exeter: Learning Matters.

Copping, A. (2010) 'Watching me, watching you, aha! Developing reflection and practice through the use of video'. *TEAN Journal* 1(2) December [Online]. Available at: http://bit.ly/tyfJ5M (accessed 22/3/12).

Cosh, J. (1999) Peer observations: A Reflective model. *ELT Journal*, 50(1). Oxford: Oxford University Press.

Dewey, J. (1933) *How We Think: A Restatement of the Relation of Reflective Teaching to the Educative Process*. Chicago: Henry Regney.

Ghaye, T. (2011) *Teaching and Learning through Reflective Practice: A Practical Guide for Positive Action*, 2nd ed. Abingdon: Routledge.

Ghaye, A. and Ghaye, K. (1998) *Teaching and Learning through Critical Reflective Practice*. London: David Fulton.

Gibbs, G. (1988) *Learning by Doing: A Guide to Teaching and Learning Methods*. Oxford: Further Educational Unit, Oxford Polytechnic.

Medwell, J. (2005) *Successful Teaching Placement*. Exeter: Learning Matters.

Mooney, C. and Fletcher, M. (2007) *Primary Mathematics: Audit and Test*, 3rd ed. Exeter: Learning Matters.

Schön, D. (1983) *The Reflective Practitioner: How Professionals Think in Action*. New York: Basic Books.

Schön, D. (1996) From technical reality to reflection in action. In R. Edwards, A. Hanson, and P. Raggatt (eds) *Boundaries of Adult Learning*. London: Routledge.

Sharp, J. and Byrne, J (2007) *Primary Science: Audit and Test*. Exeter: Learning Matters.

Ward, J. and McCotter, S. (2004) Reflection as a visible outcome for pre-service teachers. *Teaching and Teacher Education*, 20: 243–57.

Zeichner, K. and Liston, D. (1996) *Reflective Teaching: An Introduction*. Hillsdale: Lawrence Erlbaum Associates.

4. Using children's talk as a basis for reflective practice
Nick Clough

Learning Outcomes

By the end of this chapter you will have developed:
- skills in evaluating and reviewing classroom interactions within a case study involving trainee teachers and teachers working together to develop reflective practice;
- critical skills in creating a rationale for reflective practice that is based in the literature of pupil talk for learning;
- skills in planning, implementing and evaluating a reflective practice process that is shared with the class teacher with whom you are working on placement.

Introduction

This chapter explores a way into reflective practice that can be initiated within the time-frame of your lesson. The argument made is that reflection is inseparable from practice – because teachers are already engaged thinking about their actions. What is needed is a practicable framework that brings actions and critical thinking together in a purposeful way in the immediate classroom situation. The conclusion drawn is that very often the spoken words used by children in their learning discussions with you and with other children represent the most immediate and accessible resource available to support you in responsive critical review of their learning and of your professional practice. The development of your reflective practice can emerge naturally through focusing on what children are saying in your lessons and how they talk together as they grapple with the material and problems that you have introduced.

Research Focus

This chapter draws on selected episodes from local case study material within a nationwide TDA-funded Initial Teacher Training 'Leading Partners' initiative shared between the Department of Education at the University of the West of England, Bristol and some of its partner schools (see Clough, 2010). As the project developed over a period of two years, within the local partnership it adopted the title of 'Improving reflective practice through shared attention to children's learning'. The intended impact of the local project was to:

$\rightarrow$

- build on what trainees had learned about the value of children's talk within mathematical investigations during centre-based training;
- encourage trainees to promote children's mathematical talk during investigations and to engage in critical evaluation of that talk;
- enhance trainees' understanding of the significance of children's talk for learning;
- engage trainees and teachers together in reflective practice that leads to their professional development.

The local project in Bristol was built around a series of meetings between the teachers and trainees involved in the project that took the form of a sustained action – reflection cycle, as follows:

- Initial meeting of trainees and the teachers with whom they were placed to explore the role of talk in learning though first-hand engagement in mathematics activities and problem-solving activities. Opportunity to plan first classroom activities.
- First feedback meeting to share reflections on the first classroom activities and to support plans to evaluate children's talk during lessons.
- Reciprocal visits to each other's classroom to observe and reflect on children's talk in mathematics lessons.
- Second feedback meeting to share reflections on subsequent classroom activities and to reflect on the impact on practice that comes from focusing on children's talk in mathematics lessons.

For the purposes of this chapter, selected case study material from the project will provide illustration of three elements of a form of reflective practice that is predicated on children's talk. These are found to be effective within the examples of trainees' work that are shared and it is argued that they should also be prioritised in your own work in the classroom.

First, it is emphasised that reflective practice becomes purposeful when it is 'talk informed' – that is, when it includes a focus on what children communicate verbally during your lessons. Second, the examples illustrate how this focus on children's talk should take account of the social context of the discussion so that the impact of the various interactions is better understood. Thus the data presented here support the developing argument that reflective practice should be 'interaction focused'. Third, it is recommended that reflective practice that focuses on talk should not be a solitary process for you as a trainee but should develop through dialogue with other teachers and supporters who are engaged with the children's learning, as well, of course, through studying research findings from other related enquiries. In this respect it is recommended that reflective practice should be 'communally theorised' so that it can contribute to the professional development of the teaching team in the school and to the achievement of targets that the school has identified.

$\rightarrow$

The sections in this chapter provide a focus on these three elements of reflective practice.

- Reflective practice that is talk informed.
- Reflective practice that is interaction focused.
- Reflective practice that is communally theorised.

In this chapter, data from the research described above are used to illustrate the developing reflective practices of four trainees, Jenny, Alice, Maggie and Sam, as documented during their final placements. Although the case studies use a mathematics context, the principles that are being discussed can be seen across the primary curriculum and beyond.

Talk-informed reflective practice

This section begins with case studies from Jenny's and Alice's classrooms. The materials are introduced to raise questions in your mind about the value of a form of reflective practice that is initiated and informed through a focus on children's talk during lessons. Following the case studies, you will be asked to reflect upon the value of focusing on children's talk during lessons as a form of reflective practice.

The case study below is illustration of how the issue of children's classroom talk became a focus for attention in this extract from a discussion between a trainee, Jenny and her school-based mentor during the latter stages of her practice in a Year 1 class. You may recognise some of these issues from your own experience.

Case Study: Jenny reflects on Peter's understanding

Mentor   Whose learning do you think we should focus our attention on?

Jenny   The one I am particularly thinking of is Peter, who is Polish. He speaks Polish at home and is learning English here in the classroom. ... Quite often the end results in his books make it look like he does not understand much at all. When we did the activity following the Bear Hunt project, he realised that his own hands were a way of measuring. We drew round the children and measured with their handspans. First he measured how big he was with hands, and then he demonstrated to the others what he had done – he counted his handspans out loud. But if that had been on paper, he would not have communicated it at all. Oracy in maths is a way of getting over that barrier for him.

Jenny is drawing on her observation of the child's communications with other children during an activity to raise questions about how we assess their understandings and applications of knowledge. A particular question about Peter

$\rightarrow$

was emerging in her mind as she had noted that it was recorded in the assessment files that he was only able to manipulate numbers up to ten. This led Jenny to share her thoughts on how she might develop her work further with the class.

Jenny   *In this class there are three groups that are quite low ability. One thing I have noticed is that some of the ones that have been judged as lower ability, when they are talking they show that they understand more than I had expected. But when they try to put this on paper, or when they are trying to understand instructions from the books, that's where they actually falter. However, when you have a conversation with them their mathematical language and their knowledge is actually good.*

Jenny described how she had been inspired by what she had learned from the first planned feedback meeting in the project.

An early years trainee, Alice and the teacher had together used Post-it notes to record in writing some short commentaries from the children as they were engaged in learning. In this way they had recorded how children expressed mathematical concepts during their engagement in mixed ability groups in a planned activity 'constructing castles'. This activity had taken place in both inside and outside environments, with recycled materials and other resources including large and small fabricated solid shapes. The adults asked simple questions about what they were doing and what they were making. Here are some typical verbatim responses from the children which Alice and the teacher shared with the other trainees and teachers involved in the project.

Case Study: Alice focuses on high-quality talk to change her teaching approach

Child outside:	We are building a castle. This is the floor.
Child cutting a zig-zag:	Big, small, big, small it makes a pattern!
Child constructing with Lego:	I'm making pyramids. I saw them in a book. I'm showing the others how to make one.
Stephen's castle:	Mine's going to have a big tower. People could poke their heads out of the window, you could climb up the towers until you get in through one of the holes and then you will be king. That's the top of the castle.
Ella's castle:	I'm trying to make the stairs. You can climb up inside and the princess and the queen and the people who live in this castle look up. That's the stairs.

→

Together the trainee, Alice, and her teacher characterised the words of the children as high-quality talk which represented, in some cases through narrative talk, their understanding of the spatial relationships within the structures that they were creating and imagining. They argued that high-quality talk was not just about learning the names of the 3D shapes, though there was evidence here that they were engaging with this. They argued that one form of high-quality talk (discursive, narrative, directional) was supporting another form of high-quality talk (distinguishing, identifying, naming) and vice versa. These reflections led to further consideration of children's learning in mixed ability groups which were reported at the second feedback session as follows.

The Early Years teacher and Alice wrote this reflective account together about their observations.

> At first one or two children took control but later it got more balanced. Some children have shared experience and show kindness to each other in small groups. The more able do support the less able. There is less frustration when the emphasis is on what they can communicate through talk. It has been really good. It has changed the way we will do our maths – we will now introduce more mixed ability grouping. We are now talking to Year 1 about what the Reception children are now used to in maths. A key point is that we are doing little investigations in the maths lesson, not large-scale investigations that are too difficult to bring to a conclusion.

This case study material is included here to illustrate how within the framework provided by the project, attention to the utterances of children led naturally to a form of shared reflective practice that supported not only open consideration of what the children understood about the content of the lesson but also about the social organisation of teaching and learning in the classroom. When this critical commentary was disseminated as part of the project, it led Jenny to consider how she herself might organise a mathematics session involving Peter.

Case study: Jenny learns more about Peter's understanding

Jenny   We are doing multiples this week and I have told the children that we have a request from the bear factory to make waistcoats for teddy bears – so I have changed it round so that they are working in mixed ability groups. They are working out how many eyes they will have to order as well as the buttons for the waistcoats.

Mentor   That sounds interesting, as the children are not used to mixed ability groupings in maths lessons. Perhaps you could get a record of how the children, and particularly Peter, use language during this lesson, and how you intervene with them.

$\rightarrow$

| Jenny | I am on my own as the teacher is away – so it is difficult to teach and listen to all the children's talking at the same time. However, I will use a digital recorder to keep a record of some key passages in the lesson. |

The recording of a key passage during supported group work in the lesson was useful to Jenny when she reflected on Peter's achievements during the task. She was able to listen again to what he said to check if her first impressions had been right, to see if progress he had seemed to make was true. A transcript of the whole teaching and learning interlude is presented here. However, it should be noted that Jenny relied for her own reflection process on notes she had made about Peter's verbal contribution to the lesson.

Jenny	We need to work out how many waistcoats we can make for these bears with these buttons. Peter, look this way. Each bear needs to have five buttons on his waistcoat. Five buttons. On his waistcoat, like this. These are all the buttons that we can find. How are we going to find out?
Ian	How many bears do we have?
Jenny	We need to find out how many waistcoats we can make. I am not sure. We can only make as many as – these are all the buttons that we have.
Jake	I remember how many bears there was.
Jenny	That was when we were putting the eyes on the bears. Let's have a look at these buttons.
Jake	Four, three.
Jenny	We have all these buttons and there needs to be five buttons on each waistcoat.
Ian	There is going to be loads of bears you know. I think five.
Peter	I'm took all these.
Jenny	Do you need some help?
Sarah	Oy! Oy! Oy! You are taking all of these.
Jenny	What do you think we need to do to work it out. I don't know. How many have you got there? Good boy.
Sarah	I found a pair.
Jenny	Aha, aha, I thought you were ...
Ian	I got twenty-one.
Ambreen	Hang, on I've got ten.
Jenny	So what can you do with ten, Ambreen? How many bears could you give waistcoats to?
Ambreen	Um, Um. I have got two fives in my hand.

$\rightarrow$

Ian	I've got twenty-one.
Jenny	How many bears, Ambreen?
Ambreen	Two.
Jenny	How many do you think you could do, Ian? With twenty-one. How many waistcoats could you make?
Ambreen	I have ten.
Jake	Nineteen.
Jenny	If each bear had to have five.
Jake	Nobody nick mine any more.
Milly	I've got five.
Jenny	How many could you do if each bear had to have five on his waistcoat, Ian?
Jake	I've got three fives.
Peter	Seven, eight, nine, ten, eleven, twelve, thirteen,
Jenny	How many have you got, Peter.
Peter	One, I think one.
Jenny	Peter, you need to listen to each other so that you can hear what the others are doing.
Peter	One, two, three, four, five, six, seven, eight, nine, ten, eleven, twelve, thirteen.
Jenny	If every bear, Peter, had to have five, if one bear needs to have five, how many waistcoats could you make? So one waistcoat has to have five. Look, like this. There are five here. How many have you got left?
Peter	One, two, three, four, five, six, seven, eight.
Jenny	So we can take these five for another waistcoat. So now, we have two waistcoats. What have you got left?
Peter	One, two, three.
Jenny	How many more do you need now to make another waistcoat? We need five and we've got three. How many more do we need?
Peter	Two more.
Jenny	Good. You need two more. How many can you make now?
Peter	One, and one and one, three.

Jenny made several observations about this teaching and learning interlude during the final evaluation stages of the project, demonstrating that she had the capacity to engage in reflective practice that can lead to critical review of her work. She was

→

most struck that Peter had counted out loud up to 13 as he handled the buttons and that his counting corresponded exactly to the buttons that he had. Previously she had only heard him count to eight as reflected in the school records. She also observed that with careful questioning and support he could cope with subdividing 13 buttons and that he could add on a remainder to make up another set of five. It was not just she who was impressed. The next morning Peter's mother reported that he had talked to her at home about his maths lesson – for the first time ever! She reported that Peter had actually said that he likes maths. Jenny herself drew a tentative conclusion that the inclusion of Peter within a group of others who were known to be more able had possibly stimulated his confidence in his own capacity. She added further comments also about high-quality talk in mathematics, as follows:

- She now understood that high-quality talk in mathematics is less about the expression through language of perfectly formed mathematical ideas and more about the practice of mathematical reasoning skills.

- She had previously thought that the development of communication and language skills for this age range could be best supported through a separate programme that focuses attention on these skills. She has now begun to think that such skills should be developed through discussions within subject lessons such as mathematics and science.

- She has begun to question the level of understanding of those who have been identified as more able and prefers to make assessments in relation to what children are able to demonstrate orally.

Jenny comments:

Also the children who are more able and are very good at literacy, actually their talk was sometimes OK but their actual mathematical understanding was not always there. So using oracy has been a good way of judging their understanding too – by listening to what they can explain as opposed to reading the final result in their books. It is possible that when they have all sat on the high ability table that one person knows the answer and the others are just copying it down. The discussions really did differentiate their abilities as well.

The need for reflective practice to be 'talk informed' – summary

These materials have been introduced to raise questions in your mind about the value of a form of reflective practice that is initiated and informed through a focus on children's talk during lessons. We have seen how Jenny is reflecting at different levels about her practice and that the sharing of these reflections is enabling her to develop her approaches within the classroom. She is now arguing a case based on her observations that children's talk may be seen as a representation of their capacity for mathematical thinking. This may seem an obvious point but importantly it is leading her to consider how this principle may affect the way that teaching, learning and assessment may best be organised in her classroom.

As you read through the transcripts from the recorded cases of Jenny and Alice, you may have been struck by details that relate to your own developing practice. You should engage in discussion with your peers or trainers about what you are learning from this and what the implications are for your developing reflective practice.

Activity

Read the transcripts presented above from Jenny and Alice's classrooms. Write some notes about (1) the children's talk (2) the trainees' reflections that you think are relevant to your own developing reflective practice. Share these with your peers and trainers.

You may also include consideration of how my own summary position statement may apply to your own situation and experience.

> *One feature of reflective practice is that it should be talk informed. Recognition of the participatory rights of children (for example the UN Convention on the Rights of the Child) predisposes sensitive reflective practitioners to the content of children's communications, especially what they say. For many children, spoken words are their most direct communication channel. Thus attention needs to be paid to children's utterances and consideration given to the meanings that they are intended to convey. For this reason reflective practitioners need to develop listening, research and recording skills that allow children's verbal messages to be captured and thought about. Reflective practice also needs to include and take account of other communication devices that some children prefer or need to employ.*

Interaction-focused reflective practice

If possible, you should now read Neil Mercer's 2008 article, 'Talk and the development of reasoning and understanding', *Human Development*, 51(1): 90–100. This provides an accessible overview of recent research about the relationship between talk – and particularly what Mercer defines as 'exploratory talk' – and children's developing capacity for reasoning. He clarifies the contributions of earlier researchers to understandings in this field, including Vygotsky and Wertsch, and draws conclusions based on his own shared enquiries that are relevant to the proposal in this chapter that reflective practice should include a focus on interactions and dialogues between teachers and children and between the children themselves. He illustrates ways in which teachers may begin to promote children's shared exploratory talk that supports them not only in solving problems but also in developing collective and individual reasoning skills.

Research Focus

A summary overview of Mercer's (2008) developing understanding of exploratory talk is included here as it provides markers for you to use when you come to evaluate the examples of children's talk that are offered in this section of the chapter.

> *Our definition of exploratory talk specified a joint, co-ordinated form of co-reasoning, in which speakers share relevant knowledge, challenge ideas, evaluate evidence, consider options and try to reach agreement in an equitable manner. By incorporating both constructive conflict and the open sharing of ideas, exploratory talk constitutes the pursuit of rational decision-making through dialogue. It depends not only upon the trust established amongst partners, but also on the kind of intersubjectivity that enables them to achieve a shared understanding of the task in hand.*

> (Mercer 2008, p.9)

Mercer's analysis of his findings from a series of interventions (referenced in his article) leads him to draw a tentative conclusion that is attractive to all reflective practitioners.

> *A ... radical and intriguing possibility is that the target children improved their reasoning skills by internalising exploratory talk so that they became more able to carry on a kind of silent, rational dialogue with themselves. That is, through adult guidance and peer group practice, they became sophisticated users of language as a psychological tool, and their thinking became more dialogic.*

> (Mercer 2008, p.13)

He finishes his paper in elegant style through posing a question for the reader.

> *We need to know more of course, but in the meantime, should we hesitate in applying what we now know about the relationship between 'thinking and speech' in the improvement of our educational systems?*

> (Mercer 2008, p.16)

The continuing argument in this chapter is that children's talk and interactions during lessons provide a most valid base for purposeful reflective practice. Evidence from the case study presented in this section provides illustration of children's capacity for such collective reasoning and of the ways in which Maggie, a trainee teacher, has begun to review her responsibilities as a teacher. There is evidence, too, of ways in which children are themselves becoming reflective learners.

The lesson emerged from the same 'action – reflection cycle' that is outlined in the description of the Bristol project at the beginning of the chapter.

Case Study: Maggie learns the value of talk in mathematics

The task that Maggie and her teacher devised involved groups of children of mixed ability in:

- designing 3D packaging that best protects biscuits when (1) dropped and (2) thrown;

- communicating findings – justifying their decisions about which 3D shape offers the best protection.

The shapes that they were testing were: rhombic prism, cube, cuboid, cone, cylinder, pyramid, pentagonal prism and dodecahedron. They immediately engaged in the activity and evidenced capacity to communicate their approaches to solving the problem using appropriate vocabulary and relevant understandings.

An example of the resulting evidence is represented here in the form of a transcript of a group of children interacting in Maggie's lesson.

Handina	Let's do a cylinder.
Ajit	It will roll and might hit things so then it [the biscuit] might break.
Sam	I think it will be strong as it's not just a rolled-up piece of paper, it has circles on the end.
Ajit	Yes, but another reason why I don't think it will be strong is that it's thin, now I think a cuboid might be quite strong.
Marie	Yeah, a cuboid might be really strong as it won't roll and if you hit it like that (*hits it on the sides of the cuboid*) it won't do any damage to the biscuit.
Sam	Yes, but there is more space for it to move, for the biscuits to move.
Handina	Let's do a pentagonal prism and a cuboid.

Children were given examples of the board of different-shaped packaging, one being Toblerone in a pentagonal prism shape.

John	Is a pentagonal prism that one that has Toblerone in it? Because biscuits are not usually triangle.
Sam	Yeah, but if there are biscuits in there when it's rolling, they are not moving because they are touching the sides as they are the same shape, they are not going anywhere.
Ajit	Yes, but I think a cuboid because it's pretty much the same but it won't roll.
Handina	Yeah, I think a cuboid because it won't roll.
Sam	Yes, but I don't think the biscuit will fit.

→

Sam	OK, let's test a pentagonal prism and cuboid.
Ajit	What is a pentagonal prism?
Sam	It is like a cylinder but with edges. It looks like this. (*Shows example of pentagonal prism.*)
Ajit	Oh, OK I think that it will be good.
John	OK, two shapes, I think we should do a cylinder and a pentagonal prism.
Marie	I'd say the cylinder is quite good as it rolls and keeps the biscuit in the shape.
Sam	I agree, I think it will be good because it will roll and the biscuits are round so will be the same shape as the packaging.
Ajit	I think we have chosen, the cylinder and the pentagonal prism. I think they are good choices and if we work together as a team it will go well.

Each group states which two shapes they have chosen. A lot of the groups have chosen to test a cylinder.

Ajit	I think we shouldn't do a cylinder as a lot of the groups have chosen to do that one, I think we should do a cuboid.
Handina	Yeah and no one has chosen the cuboid.
Sam	OK.
Ajit	OK, so we are decided we shall do a cuboid instead of a cylinder, and the good news is that no one has done either of our shapes.

The children test the packaging by throwing.

Handina	That one sounded like it broke.
Ajit	I have a feeling that it broke too.
Sam	I think that it went very well.

They open the packaging.

Ajit	They're perfect, I think it went well.
Sam	I can't believe that they [biscuits] are perfect.
Handina	Not a single crack.
Ajit	Not a single crack. I think I can give this 100 per cent.
Handina	100 per cent.
Ajit	No cracks at all.
Handina	They were both really good.

$\rightarrow$

Marie	I think they both went well, really good packaging.
Ajit	I think they are really good packaging too.

Later Maggie and her mentor reflected on this teaching interlude.

Mentor   What are you learning yourself from these activities?

Maggie   I am learning about using investigational activities within the mathematics classroom to firstly promote the use of talk, and secondly to give more control of the lesson over to the children. I believe that this has shown to be an effective way of promoting high-quality talk, and hope to continue the use of group investigations within my future practice. It was great just to allow children to work together and talk about maths instead of being asked to continually answer questions – to be able to use what they have learned – it is important. The investigations gave them a purpose and motivated them and gave them something to think about. It was not necessary to have an answer. I had no idea which shape would be best. It was no use them asking me. They knew I did not know – we were finding out together. They were taking control.

Mentor   How has this helped you develop your mathematics subject knowledge?

Maggie   I am learning that the knowledge of maths should be seen as a whole. I had it down as shape and then using data handling. Then the children brought in all these other aspects, for example, halving, averaging, division, addition, percentages, I did not mention percentages at all. When I mentioned they could rate the success out of 100, maybe I thought about it but I never thought they would. They were outside in their little groups – saying this looks like about 60 per cent of the biscuit has been broken. There is 40 per cent left. When they were rating they would say I would give this 90 out of 100 so 90 per cent – they were linking it themselves. I was shocked! I was not expecting that. I had not thought they could use or apply it. I began to see maths as cross mathematical. I think this is pedagogical.

Mentor   What has been the main impact on the children's learning experience?

Maggie   They were engaging in exploratory talk – it is what Mercer has written about. They are beginning to be able to challenge each other and to engage in joint consideration and joint agreement. But they do actually challenge each other, for example about which shape they should use. They are helping each other to reason – they are giving each other their own reasons, saying I agree but I think this. Not just agreeing but engaging with each other as they were thinking about the solid shape and its properties. They had a choice the next day and changed their

$\rightarrow$

minds! It is interesting – they are only seven, eight years old and yet they are involved in discussion, they were listening to each other. The more able were helping the others. They were thinking about what each other said.

Mentor   Have you engaged in this way of working in your earlier placements?

Maggie   During the sessions at the University we have been learning about investigations in mathematics and Rich Maths activities. I am now much more confident about this approach but I have not used it before. I did not practise it in my first placement because of my own confidence level and also because of what I met in school. I did not try it in my second practice either for the same reasons. Really looking back I do not know why I did not try it out before but until now I did not have the confidence. The project has given me the confidence to try it out. I have learned that it is not new – it has been around since Cockcroft – or before then. Even in the 1960s and 1970s people were talking about talk across the primary curriculum and it is strange that it has not been taken up. People have been saying that talk in mathematics is a good thing – but you don't really see it. It is not the norm as I have found it. It is crazy.

The need for reflective practice to be 'interaction focused' – summary

This case study was introduced to raise questions in your mind about the value of a form of reflective practice that results from a focus on interactions in the classroom. We have seen how Maggie is reflecting at different levels about her practice and that the sharing of these reflections is enabling her to develop her approaches within the classroom. She is now arguing a case that is informed by her detailed observations that when children are given space to investigate and solve problems, their collaborative exploratory talk allows them to support each other and develop their powers of skills and reasoning – in the way that Mercer argued (see research focus above). As in Mercer's examples, the children are engaging in exploratory talk and are applying knowledge and skills that they bring to the learning. Maggie is considering how this principle of allowing opportunity for collaborative talk might influence her future practice.

As you read through the transcripts from Maggie's experience presented above, you may have been struck by details that relate to your own developing practice. You should engage in discussion with your peers or trainers about what you are learning from this and what the implications are for your developing reflective practice.

Activity
Read the transcripts presented above from Maggie's classroom. Write some notes about (1) the children's talk and (2) Maggie's reflections that you think are relevant to your own developing reflective practice. Share these with your peers and trainers.

You may also include consideration of how my own summary position statement may apply to your own situation and experience.

Another feature of reflective practice is that it can be interaction focused. A feature of children's voice and utterance is that it emerges within a social context which engages other children. Exploratory talk that represents an instance of learning is of prime interest to those who are developing pedagogical skills as beginning teachers. Such instances might be a 'heureka' moment when a new understanding, skill or value is seemingly acquired but these should not overshadow the representation of understandings, skills and values that are being reapplied and consolidated in a new context. Reflective practice provides insights into interactive pedagogies that engage children in new and continuing learning.

Reflective practice as an opportunity for communal theorising

Research Focus

Alexander (2008) identifies principles, repertoires and indicators that characterise what he calls dialogic practice, many of which resonate strongly with the assertion in this chapter that reflective practice should be talk informed, interaction focused and communally theorised. In an important section entitled 'From interactive whole class teaching to dialogic teaching', he argues that 'dialogue can take place in any organisational context. It commands attention to the power of talk in teaching and learning wherever it is used' (p.22).

In the final section he proposes a set of principles, repertoires and indicators for dialogic teaching that you can use now as a basis for evaluating the case study material presented in this chapter, and also that you set for your own reflective practice as it develops from reading this chapter. Alexander provides five descriptors as follows (p.38):

Dialogic teaching is:

1. *Collective*: teachers and children address learning tasks together, whether as a group or as a class.

2. *Reciprocal*: teachers and children listen to each other, share ideas and consider alternative viewpoints.

3. *Supportive*: children articulate their ideas freely without fear or embarrassment over 'wrong' answers; and they help each other to reach common understandings.

4. *Cumulative*: teachers and children build on their own and each other's ideas and chain them into coherent lines of thinking and enquiry.

$\rightarrow$

5. *Purposeful*: teachers plan and steer classroom talk with specific educational goals in view.

There is evidence from the case study material and readings in the next part of this chapter that such dialogic principles can be applied to teachers' own learning and development. Reflective practice has richer outcomes when it provides opportunity for practitioners to share and develop ideas together, to review and develop their practice through a critical and dialogic process. This is most powerful when the emerging rationales are evidence based (for example, based on what we learn from the children's talk) and jointly theorised.

There is evidence from the case study material and readings in this chapter that the outcomes of reflective practice are enhanced when it provides opportunity for practitioners to share and develop ideas together. The reflection process can lead to a review of practice and this is most powerful when the justifications are evidence based (for example, on what we learn from the children's talk) and jointly theorised.

Case Study: Maggie reflects on discussion opportunities

Maggie commented in this way about the discussions that were made possible through the planned stages of reflection in the project.

Talking helps us to think as well. I found that from this project. I have been able to talk which has helped me to develop my thinking about my practice. The planned meetings enabled me to think about it more. I usually don't take this much time to think about what I have been doing. This has been the first time I have had opportunity to critically reflect and talk and then think about it more.

Case Study: Sam uses Lesson Study to work collaboratively

In the second phase of the project 'Improving reflective practice through shared attention to children's learning', Lesson Study was adopted as a method as the approach matched well with the best practice identified in the first stage. More can be learned about 'Lesson Study' from Pete Dudley and Elizabeth Gowing's chapter in this book. The version that was implemented in the second phase of the project specified that the following activities were essential.

• Identification of a learning need – with a focus on the learning of a particular group of children.

• Finding out about current good practice in this area and new research.

• Using this to plan lessons collaboratively.

• Teaching and observing collaboratively.

$\rightarrow$

- Analysis of successes and things that didn't go as expected.
- Refining and developing the practice in the classroom.
- Sharing next steps and making plans.

It can be noted that the final three bullet points involve a form of reflective practice that is shared between the trainee and the teacher. Part-way through the placement Sam, the trainee, commented:

> *The main difference here has been that I have shared the reflection with my class teacher during and after each lesson. One of us has acted as lead teacher while the other has documented what children have said during the activities we have set up. We have focused particularly on a group of middle-achieving boys who have become stuck. In my previous practices I have had to go away at the end of the week to plan over the weekend – only to find that my teacher has drawn different conclusions about what we should do next. Here we are making these decisions all the time and this means that the reflection and planning processes are more connected. We are learning together about what the children are understanding through noting and discussing the children's talk during their activities*

Activities

Activity 1: You may consider how my own summary position statement may apply to your own situation and experience.

> *Reflective practice is characterised as not only situational (arising from the immediacy of the learning interlude) but also as a shared act – involving other teachers and education workers, those with responsibility in the home setting and the children themselves. It is a dialogic process that contributes not only to the teacher's professional understandings but also to what is communally understood about each child's continuing learning needs. Insights from reflective practice can contribute to wider discussions that safeguard children's educational entitlements.*

Activity 2: Consider how you can use the opportunity of your own placement for a form of reflective practice that also engages the class teacher in jointly theorising about how to enhance the learning experiences in the classroom. The following framework may support your discussions with the class teacher.

Through discussion with the class teacher with whom you are placed, negotiate a focus for shared reflective practice during an identified period in your professional placement. Identify a learning focus for this reflective practice that is already listed in the school development (improvement) plan. Identify a group of learners whose talk and utterances you will draw on as a basis for your reflective practice. Together make plans to co-teach and co-reflect for a series of lessons during which you develop understanding of this group's engagement in this area of learning through what they say/communicate as they are engaged in the activities. Allocate alternating roles to yourselves – one acting as leader of learning, the other as documenter of children's talk during each lesson. Together reflect on the new evidence base that you are developing about these learners, how this evidence might be shared with others (including the children) and the consequences for subsequent lessons.

Activity 3: If you have valued the proposal in this chapter that children's talk provides an appropriate base for reflective practice, then you could consider the joint use of the 'reflective practice wheel' presented in Figure 4.1. Starting at 'point zero' in the centre of the wheel, plot your developing reflective practices through your period of work together. As you evaluate the outcomes for your shared reflective practice, you could include consideration of the need to keep a balance between the eight related activities represented on the wheel.

In what ways is your practice providing opportunities for each of the eight components identified?

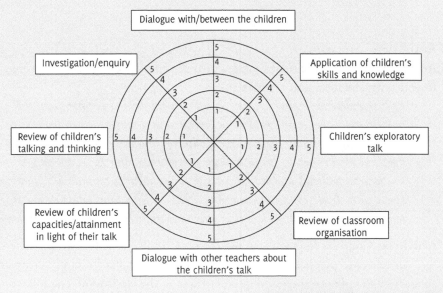

Figure 4.1: The reflective practice wheel

Learning Outcomes Review

You will have noted that reflective practices are not value free and that particular purposes can be built into this professional practice. In this chapter, an ethical stance of a kind has been adopted that will certainly be contested by some educationalists –

that teachers should relate their reflective practices to a learning/assessment process that draws on children's talk and communication during lessons.

Two kinds of criticism will arise. At one level it may be understood that reflective practice should be predicated on wider concerns than interactions within the classroom and that it should raise basic/primary questions, for example about the purposes of education itself. In the framework that is presented here, such questions are presented as secondary concerns, with the effect that discussions about what constitutes worthwhile learning occur in relation to children's talk in tasks that have been predetermined by adults to promote discussion, engagement and interaction.

Thus we could ask whether children should be involved in other kinds of activity than designing packages for chocolate biscuits – a consumerist process associated with an unhealthy foodstuff that is not wholly locally sourced. At another level participants may claim that learning to capture children's utterances is not a principal skill that trainee teachers should be developing, given the other professional pressures involved in becoming a teacher. Thus it is appropriate to ask the following questions.

Self-assessment questions

1. To what extent is the focus on children's talk supporting your developing reflective practice?
2. How would your engagement with other ethical and philosophical questions further support developments in your reflective practice?

Discussions of these questions will support you in addressing the other learning outcomes identified.

Further Reading

Your considerations of the questions above would be supported through a reading of Winch, C. and Gingell, J. (2008) *Philosophy of Education: The Key Concepts*. London: Routledge.

References

Alexander R. (2008) *Towards Dialogic Teaching: Rethinking Classroom Talk*. Dialogos: York.

Clough, N. (2010) Improving ITE through attending to children's Mathematical talk. *Leading Partners in Mathematics*. Pilot project – University of the West of England, Bristol. Available from: http://eprints.uwe.ac.uk/12927/2/Clough_2010_Improving_ITE_through.pdf (accessed 28/3/12).

Mercer, N. (2008) Talk and the Development of Reasoning and Understanding. *Human Development*, 51(1): 90–100.

DfES (2008) *Improving Practice and Progress through Lesson Study*. London: National Strategies.

Winch, C. and Gingell, J. (2008) *Philosophy of Education: The Key Concepts*, 2nd ed. London: Routledge.

5. Using coaching as a tool for reflection
Mike Pezet

Learning Outcomes

By the end of this chapter you will be able to understand:
- the relationship between coaching and reflective practice;
- what coaching is;
- coaching skills;
- the similarities and differences between coaching and mentoring;
- coaching processes and frameworks;
- coaching as a tool for reflection with:
  - peers
  - self
  - pupils.

Introduction

Within the ever-changing and increasing demands on teachers' time, coaching has the potential to offer efficient reflective practices.

Both coaching and reflective practice aim for the same outcome: the development of higher order thinking and problem-solving skills. Both approaches consider ownership, accountability and responsibility as key elements in the development and application of higher order reasoning. In education, enhanced professional practice is built from the development of autonomy, expertise and pedagogical reasoning.

Reflective practice can, however, be undermined by lack of clarity; Murray et al (2008) observed that in the absence of clear roles, or leadership, reflective discussions were unfocused. Coaching demands clear roles, structure and expectations in order to be effective.

This chapter focuses on how coaching can be used as a tool for reflection. The chapter begins with an overview of coaching and reflective practice, followed by an overview of coaching, coaching skills and the similarities and differences of coaching and mentoring, before moving on to an overview of coaching processes and frameworks followed by their use as a reflective tool with peers, self and children.

What is coaching?

Over the past 20 years coaching has spread as a managerial and learning tool across sectors such as education, health, finance and personal growth, to name a few. Indeed coaching, along with mentoring, has been heralded with 'manic optimism' (Gibson, 2005) which may cause some to question the value of coaching.

At a fundamental level coaching is, however, a problem-solving process: how to get from A to B. For example, B might be 'I want to manage classroom behaviour more effectively', and A is 'because currently I feel out of my depth'. The skill lies in acting within the broad principles of coaching to help the person problem solve how they might, and how they want, to get from A to B.

I suggest the following are a set of broad principles of coaching.

- To build resourcefulness and autonomy through people discovering the solutions within themselves.
- The coach does not know or have the 'right' answer.
- The person has the answers within the context of their aspirations, perceptions, experience, and so on, to solve the problem, not the coach.
- To build self-motivation through ownership of the goals and solutions.
- To develop new insights and alternative approaches by stimulating and challenging thinking.
- You cannot coach somebody who does not wish to be coached.

Coaching within these principles can be demanding as it may require rethinking how one helps another to learn and grow.

Research Focus

In her research of teachers learning to coach, Gibson (2005, p 77) observed:

> it is probable that every experienced teacher who takes on a coaching role will experience a specific set of specific and challenging issues requiring learning and growth... learning how to coach effectively is likely to be at least as challenging and complex an endeavor as learning to teach is, and requires professional and cognitively demanding work.

Part of the cognitively demanding work of coaching is the capacity to work in a non-evaluative manner yet still challenge and stimulate the coachee's thinking. The key is in building a relationship based on transparency, trust and safety (covered in the coaching processes section later in this chapter). For example, Latz et al (2009) found that trust and rapport rapidly decrease if people sense they are being judged or evaluated. Managing our own judgements requires awareness of the influence they have on what we hear and what we say.

'Pushing in' and 'pulling out' knowledge

A simple method to remain aware of judgement is to think of coaching approaches in terms of 'pushing in' or 'pulling out' knowledge.

'Push in' techniques are directive and judgement based; they involve pushing your knowledge or opinions onto someone, for example telling them what to do or think. Working at the 'push' end of the spectrum I refer to as *pushing your agenda*, which means pushing your own view of what needs to be focused on, done or acted upon.

Directive approaches have their place in the development of people, perhaps in the early months of a teacher's career when there is a need to build craft skills (Sutherland, 2006). However, motivation is a factor with 'push in' approaches. For example, it can be difficult to implement someone else's idea because their confidence, experience and knowledge differ from yours. Motivation might therefore decline when the person who 'directed' you isn't available to explain or support actions.

'Pulling out' is the use of questioning and listening to draw out thoughts, perceptions and knowledge. 'Pull out' techniques are non-directive and seek to engage motivation through self-generated goals and solutions. Working at the 'pull out' end of the spectrum I refer to as *working with their agenda*. Within the conversation, this means what is focused on, opened up or acted on is largely shaped by the needs and interests of the person being coached.

Managing judgement and working within the principles of coaching means endeavouring to *work with their agenda*. Coaching with 'pulling out' techniques aims to help people develop insight into the influence their assumptions, values and beliefs have on their perceptions, the choices they make and actions they take. In doing so people develop higher order thinking, problem-solving skills and autonomy.

Coaching and mentoring

Coaching and mentoring are terms often used interchangeably; this section makes the distinction in order to help you structure reflective practice appropriately.

Activity
Do you see a difference between 'coaching' and 'mentoring'? What do you understand the difference between these terms to be? How are they similar?

Coaching and mentoring share the same aim and skill sets – the development of the individual through goal-setting, questioning and listening – but differ on a number of areas.

One area is *focus*. Mentoring is generally long term and focused on career development as well as skills development. Coaching is generally shorter term and focused on building capability and skills around specific issues or challenges.

Another area is *authority*. Mentoring is generally hierarchical; a senior, expert teacher has responsibility for guiding and developing a novice teacher into, say, the school system and craft skills. On the other hand, coaching can be by a peer or an external coach. A coach's authority is not based in 'expert' knowledge or hierarchical power but in their ability to build a climate of trust and openness through coaching skills.

Coaching always works with or seeks to understand the agenda of the 'client', for example, the issues and challenges as the 'client' sees them, by using 'pull' techniques. Mentoring can do the same but can also be driven by the mentor's agenda of what they think is best to focus on or develop.

Activity

Consider the two techniques highlighted above. Think of a situation where you have used 'push in' and 'pull out' techniques in your own professional work with colleagues and children, or where a colleague has used them with you.

Reflect on the outcomes of using pull techniques – for you, for your colleague, for children. Can you think of specific colleagues, children or situations where 'pulling out' techniques might be of benefit?

Coaching skills and processes

This section discusses how listening and questioning are core coaching skills which are key to working in a way that *works with their agenda* to 'pull out' knowledge.

Listening

In coaching, listening is conscious and active. Being listened to impacts significantly on people; they feel acknowledged, respected and assured. However, most of the time you will be selective in what you hear; you distort, misinterpret and form judgements about what is being said.

Listening actively takes skill, energy and focus. Focus means that your attention is on the person, what they are saying or not saying, the way they structure what they say, the words they use, their tone of voice and the shifts in body. Energy maintains focus and awareness of when your attention drops and needs to be brought back again.

Listening is a skill that can be learned and managed; a simple technique is to think of listening in terms of different levels of attention.

Level 1 – low level attention

At level 1 your attention is predominantly on your own thoughts; people may be talking with you but your mind is elsewhere. Signs of level 1 are little if any engagement with the conversation, distracted attention, focusing elsewhere.

Level 2 – medium level attention

Your attention is on what you hear others say as well as on your own thoughts and internal dialogue.

For example, your previous perception of the person and their credibility may lead you to begin the conversation with a preconceived idea of how it will go. You may unknowingly form judgements about whether what is being said is wrong or right or whether you've heard it before. You may drop to level 1 by daydreaming during the conversation, or find the discussion triggers a memory. You may mentally prepare your response before they've finished speaking, which is generally indicated by responses such as:

- 'Ahh yes, but...'
- 'I remember when I did that and...'
- 'If I were you I would...'
- 'What you ought to do is...'

Level 3 – high level attention

At level 3 your attention is on the speaker and you are curious about what their words mean to them. Energy is directed to all listening resources: ears, eyes, senses, intuition, and using them as a source of information (see section below, Questioning).

Your energy is used to manage your internal dialogue. We never escape the capacity to form opinions or judge about what others are saying but we can manage their influence. At level 3 you're aware of your internal dialogue but can keep it from interfering with hearing the coachee.

At level 3 you also 'hold' in mind the aims for the conversation as well as the longer-term aims of the coaching and feed these back into the conversation.

For example, the exploration of one issue may initiate a new train of disclosure from the coachee and the conversation may begin to feel tangential. At the *working with their agenda* end of the scale the coach could reintroduce the overall goals by asking, in a non-evaluative manner, 'Is the issue you just mentioned related to the goals you had for this conversation? Which was, to clarify your approach to curriculum interpretation and consider some alternatives?'

Asking in a non-evaluative manner gives the coachee the opportunity to identify connections, deepen thinking and self-evaluate any benefit of discussing the new area. Whether a relationship exists or not is determined by the coachee.

Activity
Listening at a high level takes energy and practice. Decide upon an appropriate situation where you can practise level 4 listening. Note what internal dialogue you are tempted to engage in. What strategies might you use to remain focused on the colleague or child?

Questioning

Effective questions help to 'draw out' people's knowledge and opinions in order to consider thoughts, alternate perspectives and options more deeply. This section highlights some suggestions for how you might ask questions to elicit deeper thinking.

Curiosity and interest
Some key resources for forming effective questions are using curiosity and interest. Curiosity conveys that the question came from an interest in the person and in what is being said. Curiosity can keep questions open and doesn't imply judgement or that there is a 'right' answer.

The case study below demonstrates curiosity and interest during a coaching sequence being undertaken in a session with Stuart, a placement mentor and Keera, a trainee teacher.

Case Study. Curiosity questions

Keera	I'm not happy with how I'm applying differentiation techniques in class. It makes sense, I know but on top of everything else I just don't have time to think about how to do it.
Stuart	I hear you say that differentiation makes sense and you're doing some in class, so I'm really interested to know more about the bits you're happy with.
Keera	Well, yesterday I managed to doing some craft work and had different outcomes for the different abilities. I was pleased that it worked quite well.
Stuart	That's interesting. Tell me more about what you did that enabled you 'manage' to build it into the day.

Because of her reflection, Keera realised, and gained confidence from the fact, that she did have methods for applying differentiation strategies. From the conversation she identified actions she had taken and how they might be repeated.

Keera also illustrates that it is easy to just focus on 'what is not working' as it tends to be uppermost in people's minds. In those cases the coach's skill is in not accepting the story as the 'truth' while asking questions that enable the coachee to re-evaluate what they are doing.

Beyond listening and questioning

There are a range of other techniques that can be used to stimulate people's thinking and encourage exploration.

Reflecting back
It is powerful to hear your own words reflected back in the form of an open question. For example, 'You said "energised". Tell me more.' The power lies in someone listening and raising awareness of the words you use and inviting you to discover the meaning behind them.

Summarising
Summarising captures the essence of what someone has said and checks for accuracy. For example, 'What I have heard is that you aren't feeling competent because you don't have time to thoroughly prepare, is that correct?' The power lies in hearing a story boiled to its essence.

However, if someone replied, 'No, that isn't right', what might your choices as a coach be? At the 'push' end a response might be, 'Well, that was what you said'; at the 'pull' end it might be, 'OK, what *would* you say?'

Attachment
Attachment is when you can't let go of your judgements or opinions. It may be a need to win, or to prove you're right. Attachment will undermine trust and send the message that coaching is about compliance rather than understanding. If you find you're attached to proving a point, acknowledge you are and let go.

Reframing
Reframing creates new ways of looking at a situation by feeding back statements from alternative viewpoints. For example, reframing can clarify goals such as, 'I really want to develop my classroom management', which can be fed back as, 'So, what does good classroom management mean to you?' Or, 'I feel so overwhelmed with all the deadlines' can be reframed as, 'So you'd like to get back some control? What would give you that?'

Silence
Silence is powerful; unfortunately, many people are uncomfortable with silence or pauses in a conversation, and they fill the void or feel the need to justify their question. For example, when

someone says 'I don't know', you may think that they don't have the answer. However, it can often be that the question has made them think deeply. Silence is OK; it gives people space to think beyond an initial response.

Noticing and feedback loops

Noticing is about being present and using all your senses as a source of information. Feedback loops are feeding back observations, sensations and intuitions in the form of questions. For example, you might observe that the person looks downwards quite quickly when mentioning a particular point. That could be fed back as, 'I notice you looked down suddenly when you mentioned lesson planning, I'm curious about that.'

The response might be, 'Oh, my neck was sore', in which case as a coach you move on. Or they may say, 'Did I? That's strange, I guess it's because I find it a real burden at present.'

Sensations and intuitions

Sensations and intuitions mean acknowledging your own body as a source of information. For example, you may have just been told a long story and feel confused by it. You may blame yourself for not following, and cover your 'mistake' by bluffing your way out of it. You can also use it as a source of information by asking, 'I am confused at the moment. I am curious to see if that is the same for you.'

The person may or may not be confused, but the question has been asked for exploration.

Intuition is about acting on those hunches you might have, but it is also about not being attached to whether those intuitions are accurate or not. For example, you might hear the story and 'sense' a subtext underlying it.

One approach is to interrupt and introduce a question: 'John, I just need to interrupt you, but is this about the relationship with the teaching assistant?' He may answer 'no', and so the art is to keep the question open without being attached to proving you are right. For example, 'OK, would you mind if we keep the question open for a moment? There may be a connection there; if not, I'll let it go, but can you tell me more?'

In summing up, any coaching session is about the coachee, not the coach. As a rule of thumb 70 to 80 per cent of the talking should be done by the coachee rather than the coach.

Coaching processes and frameworks

This section covers coaching processes, establishing a reflective coaching relationship and an overview of frameworks for structuring reflective coaching conversations.

Coaching typically follows a standard sequence of activities. These are:

- *Establishing the relationship, or contracting*: the key activity for establishing clarity and trust.
- *Pre-coaching session preparation*: in education contexts this might involve observation, or a

series of questions to prepare for the session.

- *Coaching session*: negotiating and focusing on the issues the coachee wishes to move forward as well as the points the coach thinks might be included.
- *Follow-up meeting*: review of learning from the session and progress since session.

Contracting the relationship

A challenge for both coaching and reflective practice is the pre-existing relationship people have with dialogue-driven learning (Sutherland, 2006). Bolton (2006) describes it as reflection as 'confession', where disclosure is high and critical enquiry low, where people like to tell their stories but few are willing to having those stories challenged.

In coaching a process called contracting is used to alter people's existing relationship with dialogue-driven learning, as well as build clarity and trust. Contracting is not a formal, legal document but a process of co-designing the relationship to ensure all parties have ownership of the goals and process and security in how it will work.

Co-designing the relationship means surfacing expectations, negotiating terms and setting goals in order to establish a productive relationship. An effective contracting process involves exploring and clarifying three areas of consideration that affect the relationship: the professionals, the procedural and the psychological.

The professional area
This comprises clarifying the purpose and focus of the relationship from all perspectives: the coachee, the coach, the induction tutor.

For example, for the induction tutor the purpose and focus might be: 'To ensure time is allocated to developing the NQT's classroom skills and effectiveness so they can quickly make a valued contribution to the children.'

For the coach it might be: 'To provide a safe time and space for the NQT to develop their practical teaching skills by integrating theoretical knowledge with classroom experiences through considered reflection.'

For the coachee it might be: 'To build confidence and competence in my teaching by reflecting on teaching practice' or 'to gain feedback on and develop my classroom management skills'.

The outcome is that both coach and coachee have the *same understanding* of the purpose and focus of the relationship.

The procedural area
As highlighted earlier, Murray et al (2008) noted the impact that lack of role clarity had on coaching discussions. Therefore the procedural area concerns practicalities such as roles, responsibilities, timescales, meeting frequency, methods of contact, cancellation notice, and who

is responsible for contacting whom. The outcome is to ensure that all are clear about the procedural aspects of the relationship.

The psychological area

The psychological area underpins the preceding two levels and is crucial in establishing trust and rapport in the relationship. The process is about negotiating meanings and concerns in order to have transparency and shared understanding.

There are no set areas to cover as each relationship is unique, however some examples are as follows.

- What does coaching and reflective practice mean to each of us?
- What do we think that looks like in practice?
- What different agendas might each of us bring to this relationship?
- Who is responsible for the outcomes?
- Is there a tension between confidentiality and responsibility to department heads?
- In order to feel open, what is confidential?
- What does challenge mean to each of us?
- What concerns does each of us have?
- How do we measure success?
- What are their aspirations as a teacher, in a year, in three years?
- How can we tell the difference between coaching and mentoring?
- How might we manage those differences?

The outcome is that trust has been accelerated through building a shared understanding of what each other expects of the relationship, what terms mean to each other, and what concerns have been addressed.

Activity

Contracting has a profound effect on the coaching relationship. For many it can be unfamiliar to talk at such depths, and may feel uncomfortable.

Consider what the coachee might be expecting prior to the initial meeting. What could be done to make the contracting beneficial for all parties?

During the contracting, what questions might be beneficial to explore, for you? For them? For the children? For the school?

Coaching frameworks as a tool for reflection

Coaching conversations occur within a framework that structures the conversation and moves problem-solving forward. The coach manages the structure; the coachee supplies the conversation content.

Research focus

In coaching literature there are numerous frameworks. Three practical and well-established frameworks are considered here. These are:

Critical incident analysis

Critical incident analysis is employed by universities to explore underlying factors in specific situations. The framework presented here was developed for schools in the north west of England by a trained psychologist and coach, Steve Kew of Fiona Reed Associates.

Solutions focus

Solutions focus is a behavioural model employed in both coaching and therapy fields. It has been developed from a range of approaches; the earliest proponent was a therapist, Steve de Shazer.

TGROW

TGROW is possibly the most well known and used coaching model and was developed from Graham Alexander's GROW model in conjunction with John Whitmore (Whitmore, 2011).

These are explored below in an education context.

Peer coaching with critical incident framework

A critical incident framework aids reflection at three levels, if need be of Van Manen's categories of reflection. These are:

- *Technical reflection*: craft skills and acceptance of given goals.
- *Interpretive reflection*: the assumptions underlying the craft skills and the consequence of application.
- *Critical reflection*: the moral and ethical concerns underlying action.

In this context a critical incident is not necessarily a dramatic event; it is an incident that is salient to you. The incident might be small but it is something that has made you question your skills, approach, beliefs, assumptions. It may relate to:

- communication
- knowledge
- skills and techniques

- culture

- relationships

- emotions or beliefs.

Steve Kew's framework systematically explores the following areas:

- *Feelings*: Identify feelings during or related to the incident being explored.

- *Assumptions*: What assumptions did you bring to the situation or underlie your approach?

- *Values*: What were your underlying values in the situation, and what values in action did the situation reveal? How did the values affect your actions?

- *Past experiences*: How may past experiences or memories have affected your actions/responses?

- *Theory*: What light does academic theory throw on the incident?

- *Alternative actions*: What alternative actions might you have taken? What would the outcomes have been?

- *Lessons learned*: What have you learned from what has happened?

- *Applying the learning*: How might you adapt this learning to other situations?

The case study below demonstrates part of the critical incident framework in action. Jane and Rob had contracted the session and the incident Rob wanted to explore was when he had shouted at the children after lunch and upset himself. As you read, be mindful of Jane's approach to the framework and working with Rob's agenda.

Case study

Jane	The incident you want to explore relates to your reaction to class restlessness after lunch, is that correct?
Rob	Yes. On that day I found myself struggling with children.
Jane	So what feelings were happening?
Rob	Well, I felt pretty low. I got a quick bite to eat and coffee and as I wasn't on playground duty I checked my lesson plans.
Jane	You said you felt pretty low?
Rob	Yes, I felt a bit drained from the morning and wanted a bit of space on my own, to recharge. The food made me feel drowsy. I checked the in-class assistant to see how they were doing. Plus I'm new to teaching I had no idea it could be so draining.
Jane	How did you feel when the children came back?
Rob	Like I hadn't caught up on my prep, my batteries seemed low, reactive, I guess.

$\longrightarrow$

Jane	I heard you say reactive, can we come back to that later? I'm curious about the feelings of the children.
Rob	Well, I noticed that depends on the weather a bit. If it is good they come in excited after running around and playing, you can see it in their faces. If it is wet and they have been inside they seem to be agitated, loads of pent-up energy. On this day they had been out and were all excited, full of happy energy.
Jane	So what feelings might be at play when all came together?
Rob	For me, 'Oh no, I am not ready, settle down, give me a chance'. For them, it might have been 'We want to keep playing'.
Jane	What happened then?
Rob	I tried to be calm, redirect their energy, but there are a few who don't want to stop. After what seemed ages I raised my voice and shouted, which affected everyone, the mood changed considerably.
Jane	You said, 'seemed like ages'; how long do you think?
Rob	Hmmm, three, four minutes.
Jane	OK, so from what I heard there had been events preceding the incident which led to a pressured few minutes.
Rob	Yes, I can see how things led to it.
Jane	I am curious about what assumptions might have been underpinning those actions and what might their influence have been?

Rob became aware of underlying assumptions for how children should behave, which differed from how they do behave. He came to appreciate that he needed to ensure some space, even just a few minutes alone, to recharge his energy. Rob also became aware of a difference between his espoused values – 'I really care about children' – and his values in action, shouting at them.

Rob decided to go back to some theoretical knowledge from his PGCE as well as seek out practical knowledge from more experienced teachers.

Activity

Identify an incident from your classroom work: something that felt difficult or had unexpectedly challenged you. With a colleague, practise the critical incident framework. Be open to following the questions that arise from the framework. Before beginning, practise contracting by discussing your roles, expectations and the process you're about to use.

Solutions focus coaching with self

Solutions focus coaching is based on the premise that small actions can create significant change and that focusing on solutions, as opposed to problems, generates momentum and motivation to change.

The solutions focus approach means focusing attention, through questioning and listening, on a number of key areas:

- The ideal outcome to the problem, expressed as clearly as possible in behavioural actions.
- Identifying the actions and behaviours that are working at present (rather than what isn't working).
- The strengths, such as values, experience, qualities, someone has and can use along with resources, such as trusted colleagues, and knowledge sources that can be used.
- The solution defined in terms of behavioural actions that incrementally move towards the ideal outcome. (De Shazer et al, 2007; O'Connell, 2009; Jackson and McKergow, 2008)

Process
Solutions focus is not linear – reflective coaching conversations rarely are. However, the distinct building blocks within a session are:

- *The broad problem and how it affects the person.* The coachee outlines the problem and the impact it is having on self and others.
- *Identify and clarify the ideal outcome to the problem.* The coachee thinks of how the situation would be different if the problem were solved or absent.
- *Scale the outcome.* The technique is to apply a solution scale between outcome and current situation (see case study below).
- *Find out what is working and build on it.* Uncover what is currently working and use that to move towards the outcome.
- *Clarify the next steps.* The coachee identifies the steps they want to take to move forward.

Challenges for the coach when using solutions focus
- Asking, exploring and defining the ideal outcome in terms of behaviours.
- Listening to the story and discerning strengths and resources to feed back to the coachee.
- Listening for descriptions built on 'feelings' and asking the coachee to describe those feelings as external behaviours. For example, 'What would you be doing if you weren't feeling isolated?'
- Asking and listening for what is working (rather than not working) and feeding this back into the conversation.
- Asking questions to help define the solution in behavioural terms and in incremental steps.

Case Study

The case study is between Alison a trainee teacher on her final placement and David, her mentor and a senior teacher with coaching skills. They are exploring classroom management in relation to the disruption some boys make when together. As you read see if you can identify the following techniques:

- Defining a future without the problem
- Scaling the problem
- Building on what is working
- Identifying strengths and resources
- Breaking the solution into incremental steps

David	We've explored some of the problem. Feeling competent and in control is important to you. Let's look at what being competent and in control would look like. Try to think of the situation as if the problem were gone. Think of what you'd be doing if the problem no longer existed.
Alison	No longer existed, heaven! If it was no longer there I'd feel relieved.
David	What would you be doing if you were feeling relieved?
Alison	I'm not sure; I guess I'd focus more on the rest of the class and lesson.
David	If you were focused on the class and lesson, what would other people see you doing? How and where might you be standing or behaving?
Alison	Standing, hmmm, I'd be in front of the class – as I think of it, I move and start to stand behind my desk as the boys get agitated. So I think I'd be in front of the desk, speaking clearly with warmth!
David	With warmth: what would they see that indicated warmth?
Alison	Well, warmth would be using individuals' names, looking at them, not referring to them as 'class'.
David	So, if you're standing in front of the class, speaking to individuals, does that relate to competence and control? Is there anything else you might be doing?
Alison	Yes, I'd certainly feel better; what else would I be doing? I suppose I would also consult with the teaching assistant more; I tend to take it on myself. So we'd jointly plan and anticipate.
David	OK, now let's take all the things that would be happening if the problem were gone. We call it the ideal outcome; give it a score of 10. Now think of a scale of 0 to 10 with 0 being far removed from the ideal outcome at 10. Where would you currently place yourself between 0 and 10?
Alison	I would say a 4 or 5.

$\longrightarrow$

David	Which is it?
Alison	4.
David	4. Tell me what is currently happening that made you place it at a 4 rather than 1 or 0?
Alison	Oh, I hadn't thought about that. I was thinking of how to get to 10. What is happening now, hmmm. Well, the teaching assistant, June, and I do sometimes anticipate and plan. I approach her to do so, we do work well together.
David	So you already plan, sounds as though you drive that, plus it sounds like June is a good resource?
Alison	Yes, definitely. When I'm preoccupied I forget to approach June, hmmm. Maybe we could be more thorough?
David	I'm also interested about the boys within that 4. Are they continually disruptive?
Alison	No, not always. They are three good friends; when separate they're good. June and I can focus on them individually. I do like them in those situations. It is when the class moves to a regrouped activity, they gravitate towards each other. In the general mêlée sometimes we miss them.
David	From what you've said you have some qualities that help you relate to the children no matter the challenges they present.
Alison	Oh, I hadn't thought about that but yes you're right. They are learning and growing and it's important to support them.
David	It sounds like a range of things are happening at the 4 mark: you taking steps to make the planning happen with June, separating the boys, relating to them well. Tell me, if we were to go one step up to a 5, what would be happening?
Alison	At a 5, well, I guess I would see June more consistently, we could be anticipating things more, particularly moves between activities. I think I'd also get alongside the boys more frequently, build a closer understanding of them.

Activity

Choose a current unresolved dilemma you have and explore the problem through using the solutions focus technique. At the end, consider what strengths and resources have been highlighted. Where do you think you predominantly focus your attention on the problem or on the solution?

> Self-coaching is not easy, as the same information or perspectives are regurgitated, leading to no new conclusions or way forward. However, by focusing on ideal outcomes and scaling the problem, solutions focus approaches can be a useful self-coaching and reflective tool. It is recommended to write rather than think your responses.

Pupil coaching with TGROW

The TGROW model of coaching is generally available in the public domain. It has developed from the GROW model developed by Graham Alexander. The model is a reflective problem-solving process. TGROW stands for:

Theme
Goals
Reality
Options
Will

The coach's skills lie in managing the overall framework of the conversation and helping the coachee reflect at the appropriate stage of the process. Like all coaching models, the process is generally dynamic and follows the conversational leads from the coachee.

For an interesting example of using GROW in a school context, visit www.cpdscotland.org.uk/what/inn/coach/workingwith/humbieprimary.asp

1. Theme

The coach's purpose in this phase is to negotiate the agenda for the session. That is achieved by listening and summarising the salient points from the coachee's description of the issue, as well as adding your own perspective. For example, a teacher, Simon, has noticed that Jenny, a Year 4 pupil, consistently seeks the toilet when it comes to written work. He decides to use a coaching approach.

Simon Jenny, I heard you say you want to be away when handwriting starts, you don't like the pencil and worry about the others. I would also like, if it is OK with you, to talk about how Mrs Jones and I might be able to help you. Which bit would you like to talk about?

Jenny The others'.

Take the lead from him/her and jointly agree the subject to be discussed.

2. Goal

The coach's purpose in this phase is twofold: first, is to establish a goal for the conversation, and second, to establish a goal for the issue being discussed. For example:

Simon   OK, Jenny, you want to talk about the others and your handwriting. We have until break ends, so that would be really helpful for you to tell me about the others and maybe, before the end, we could look at what might be different?

Jenny   They are better than me and I don't like feeling that I can't keep up.

Because coaching conversations are not linear, the goal for the issue may not be appropriate as the issue has not been sufficiently explored. An approach could be:

Simon   As we talk, can you think about how you want things to be different, or you to be different, from how things are now?'

3. Reality

The coach's purpose in this phase is to ask reflective questions that help clarify the issue, identify blocks to progress, strengths, what works, etc. Areas of reflection might be:

- *Clarifying frequency*: 'What are the times when the problem occurs with the others and the handwriting?'
- *Exceptions to the problem*: 'Are there times when the problem with the others and the handwriting doesn't happen? What is happening then?'
- *Asking people to open up*: 'Tell me more about that.'
- *Previous experience*: 'What has worked in the past with handwriting? What did you find worked really well?'
- *Inhibitor*: 'What do you think stops you?'
- *Uncovering what works*: 'What bits of working with the others and handwriting do you like? Which bits don't you like?'
- *Uncovering support*: 'Who do you feel might be of help to you?'
- *Control*: 'What bits of the handwriting problem can you control and which bits can't you control?'

In coaching sessions, the majority of a session, 50 to 60 per cent of the time should be spent helping the person explore their perceptions of reality. A technique to manage the framework of the conversation is to refer back to the session goals. For example:

Simon   You wanted to talk about the others and we've looked at it different ways. Do you feel you have some ideas for things to do differently?

This shifts focus to the next phase: options.

4. Options

The coach's purpose is to help identify options for closing the gap between the current reality and the desired outcome. Questions help explore the feasibility of the options and identify the one the person is motivated to implement.

Jenny	I really like Hannah, she helps me a lot, sitting next to her would be good. I don't want to move tables as I like the others. I like Mrs Jones, she is nice and cares. Maybe she could be near?
Simon	That's a load of ideas for the table you sit at. What about your handwriting itself?
Jenny	Hmmm, I don't like it but someone to help would be good. I could practise at break, maybe at home, but I am not sure what to do. I don't like asking for help as I think the others laugh. Maybe I could signal you for help?
Simon	Sure. I am not aware of others laughing at you. You have a few ideas there. Which works best for you and which would you actually like to do?
Jenny	I want to be able to signal you, ask for help in a way that means I am not embarrassed. I want to practise more. Could I sit next to Hannah?

5. Will

The coach's purpose is help build motivation and commitment by defining the solution in clear actions that the person has chosen to implement.

Simon	OK, which shall we do first?
Jenny	Signalling.
Simon	What do you want to do?
Jenny	Well, when their heads are down I could look up. If you see me looking, you could come over?
Simon	That sounds fine, but I may not be able to come straight over if I am busy. What could we do then?
Jenny	What if Mrs Jones also knew? She could come over?
Simon	Sounds fine. Let's talk with Mrs Jones about it.

For each option, clear achievable actions, that are congruent for the coachee, need to be defined. If time permits the coach can revisit the initial issues to work through each one.

A technique to test commitment is asking people to rate their motivation on a scale of 1 to 10, 10 being high. An answer below 7 may indicate low motivation, so a revisit to the reality phase can help clarify the reasons behind the low motivation.

At salient points, or the end of each stage or session, the coachee's reflection can be deepened by asking, 'What have you become more aware of about yourself, in relation to (for example, class, management, lesson planning, curriculum implementation), as a consequence of exploring this issue?'

Activity

Take time to reflect on the children you teach. Can you see occasions where you might want to use the TGROW approach to help them reflect and develop self reliance? Can you list the reasons that might prevent you using TGROW or coaching with pupils? What goal might you want to set yourself regarding using TGROW and coaching with pupils?

Learning Outcomes Review

This chapter has encouraged you to consider the use of coaching for reflective practice in a number of different circumstances. Of primary importance is the establishment of the coaching/reflective practice relationship by building clarity, security and trust through contracting and co-designing the relationship. The key concepts to master are using high level questioning and listening to 'pull out', rather than 'put in', knowledge in order to work with 'the coachee's agenda'. Coaching frameworks, such as critical incident or TGROW, help structure and focus the conversation in order to enable reflective dialogue and re-evaluation of perceptions.

Self-assessment questions

1. In what situations can you see coaching aiding reflective practice?
2. Identify three questioning skills.
3. Who 'owns' and is responsible for the outcomes of a coaching session?
4. What undermines the effectiveness of any coaching, reflective practice session?
5. Rate your listening skills on a scale of 1 to 10, 10 being very good. Where are you currently? What is working? What would one step up the scale look like? What would you be doing differently?

Further Reading

Passmore, J. (2007) *Excellence in Coaching*. Association for Coaching. London: Kogan Page

De Shazer, S., Dolan, Y., Korman, H., Trepper, T., McCollum, E. and Berg I.K. (2007) *More Than Miracles: The state of the Art of Solutions Focused Brief Therapy*. London: Routledge.

Whitmore, J. (2011) *Coaching for Performance*. London: Nicholas Brealey.

References

Bolton, G (2006) *Reflective Practice: Writing and Professional Development*, 2nd ed. London: SAGE.

De Shazer, S. Dolan, Y. Korman, H. Trepper, T. McCollum, E. Berg I.K. (2007) *More Than Miracles: The State of the Art of Solutions Focused Brief Therapy*. London: Routledge.

Gibson, S.A (2005) Developing knowledge of coaching. *Issues in Teacher Education*, Fall edition.

Jackson, P. and Mckergow, M. (2008) *The Solutions Focus*. London: Nicholas Brealey.

Kinlaw D.C. (1999) *Coaching for Commitment*. San Francisco: Pfeiffer Wiley.

Latz, A., Kristie, L., Spiers, N., Adams, C.M. and Pierce, R.L. (2009) Peer coaching to improve classroom differentiation: Perspectives from project CLUE. *Roeper Review*, 31:27–39. The Roper Institute.

Murray, S., Ma, X. and Mazur, J. (2008) Effects of peer coaching on teachers' collaborative interactions and students mathematics achievement. *Journal of Educational Research*, 102(3), January/February.

O'Connell, B. (2009) *Solutions Focus Therapy*. London: SAGE.

Passmore, J. (2007) *Excellence in Coaching*. Association for Coaching. London: Kogan Page.

Sutherland, J. (2006) Promoting group talk and higher order thinking in pupils by 'coaching' secondary English trainee teachers. *Literacy*, 40(2), July.

Venman, S., Denessen, E., Gerrits, J. and Kenter, J. (2001) Evaluation of a coaching programme for cooperating teachers. *Educational Studies*, 27(3).

Whitmore, J. (2011) *Coaching for Performance*. London: Nicholas Brealey.

6. Using self- and peer-assessment for reflection
Lisa Murtagh

> ### Learning Outcomes
> ....
> By the end of this chapter you will be able to:
> - plan self- and peer-assessment opportunities for children to improve their learning;
> - use self- and peer-assessment to improve your teaching and learning;
> - develop your own and children's self- and peer-assessment strategies as tools for reflecting on learning.

Introduction

This chapter will encourage you to develop your understanding of self- and peer-assessment as tools to support reflective practice. It will develop your understanding of the principles of self- and peer-assessment with regard to both your own metacognitive development and that of the children you teach.

The principles of self- and peer-assessment

In this chapter, I use the term 'assessment' as opposed to 'evaluation'. The reason for making an explicit distinction between the two terms is that, from my experience, the terms are often used synonymously with an assumption that they mean the same thing. However, it is important that you understand the discernible differences between the two. I recently asked a group of final year trainee teachers to share with me the strategies that they used with children to engage them in self- and peer-assessment. What immediately struck me was that they largely identified evaluative strategies, *not* assessment strategies. For example, they identified the following strategies.

- Children drawing smiley faces on their work to show that they understood.
- Asking children to put 'thumbs up' or 'thumbs down' to indicate the extent to which they felt that they had met the Learning Objective.

Research Focus

To explain this, I will draw on the work of Tunstall and Gipps (1996) which considers feedback. Tunstall and Gipps investigated the types of feedback given to primary students in classes in the UK, and developed a typology of teacher feedback, classifying feedback comments as evaluative or descriptive. Evaluative feedback is described as feedback that is judgemental, and an example of such feedback takes the form of comments such as 'Good' and 'Well done' written on children's work. Descriptive feedback is described as that which is competence related, and an example of such feedback would be the comment, 'Well done, Kelly. You read with really good expression. I liked the way your voice went high when you read the part of the mouse.'

Activity

Look at some children's work that you have recently marked. Can you distinguish between evaluative and descriptive feedback? Which do you tend to provide? Why?

Assessment or evaluation?

In many ways, the response of the students outlined above is unsurprising given that while many professionals in the field seem to agree on the fact that assessment is a generic component of effective teaching and learning, the term 'assessment' has been conceptualised in many different ways.

The term 'assessment', Harlen (1994) states, includes the gathering, interpreting, recording and using of information about a pupil's response to an educational task. An assessment instrument may take the form of, for example, a written test paper, an interview schedule, a measurement task using equipment or a class quiz. In addition to these more 'formal' instruments, assessments can also take the form of observing actions, listening, reading written work and studying products such as drawings and artefacts.

Activity

Look back at some of your recent teaching. Can you list the types of assessment 'instruments' that you use. Do you use a variety or do you tend to use similar ones?

Assessment serves a multitude of purposes, and arguably many of them are contradictory. For example, 'traditional' classroom assessments and reporting processes, such as tests, allow for comparison among pupils, and fulfil accountability demands but, ironically, do not necessarily provide any specific information about what the pupil has achieved. And Gipps (1994, p.3) notes that 'assessment to support learning, offering detailed feedback to the teacher and pupil, is necessarily different from assessment for monitoring or accountability purposes.' This starting point for considering the term 'assessment' highlights its very complex nature.

Formative assessment

Activity

Prior to reading the next sections, can you provide yourself with working definitions of formative and summative assessment?

Draw up a list of strategies that you use – can you separate those that you think are formative from those that are summative?

Research Focus

In efforts to address the tensions with the term 'assessment', Bloom, Hastings and Maddaus (1971) introduced the concept of 'formative assessment' to illustrate the difference between assessment to make summative evaluations and the notion that assessment can also form a central part of the teaching and learning process.

At its most simplistic level, formative assessment should support the teaching and learning process (Gipps and Murphy, 1994); however, despite this apparently clear definition, there are a number of quandaries associated with formative assessment. First, Black and Wiliam (1998) argue that much of what is described by teachers as formative assessment, is in fact 'periodic summative', whereby assessment occurs continually, but results are used, in the main, to calculate and record 'scores' or 'marks'. In this context, there may be feedback given to the learners; however, it is used largely to present them with information about their success as opposed to impacting directly upon teaching and learning. Second, much of the information on the subject of formative assessment assumes that the focus of control lies with the teacher, with pupils portrayed as passive, learning only as a consequence of the decisions made by the teacher (Dann, 2002).

Torrance and Pryor (1998, p.8) highlight the potential of the role of both teachers and pupils in formative assessment, whereby:

> The process of formative assessment could be largely teacher controlled, with teachers providing feedback to pupils on how well they have achieved particular objectives at a particular point in time, and what else they might need to do in order to improve. On the other hand, it can be argued that formative assessment should be essentially focused on the pupil experience; that it must inevitably involve pupils reflecting on what they have achieved and how they have achieved it.

Returning to the beginning of this section, you will recall that students identified specific strategies that they felt were indicative of pupils engaging in self- and/or peer assessment. Let us unpick this a little further in light of the above discussion.

> ### Activity
>
> To what extent do the students' suggested strategies ask children to reflect on what they have achieved and how they have achieved?
>
> Can you reflect on your own experiences either as a learner yourself, or a recent classroom teaching episode you have observed or taught, and identify other examples of *self-evaluation* that you considered at the time to be *self-assessment?*

The purpose of asking you to examine the language of 'evaluation' and 'assessment' is to encourage you to begin to consider how you can develop children as metacognitive learners. Put simply, I am suggesting that evaluation is a process used to determine the quality of a performance or outcome – to judge 'worth' or 'merit' – whereas assessment has the potential to do more.

> ### Activity
>
> In the classroom, do you encourage self-assessment or self-evaluation with your pupils? Why?

Pupil self-assessment

Pupil self-assessment is a crucial feature of formative assessment, and through involving pupils, there is evidence to suggest that their progress, persistence and self-esteem improve.

Black and Wiliam (1998) assert the importance of self-assessment with regard to developing children's learning. However, Clarke (2001) suggests that children need training to be able to self-assess, monitor and manage their own learning. She suggests that children need to be trained:

- how to answer a self-assessment question;
- how to think and get into the habit of linking questions with the learning intention.

At the heart of Clarke's suggestions are teachers:

- sharing learning intentions with pupils and reiterating them;
- modelling responses;
- allowing 'thinking time'.

Clarke also illustrates how pupil self-assessment impacts upon teachers. She describes how teachers gain a greater insight into children's learning needs and make links with feedback and planning, thus highlighting how valuable self-assessment can be as an assessment tool, with information being very clearly used to impact on future planning.

Case Study: Encouraging children's self- and peer- assessment

Sandeep was a trainee working in a Year 5 class of 27 children, and chose to introduce new and robust self/peer-assessment strategies to address under-achievement in non-narrative writing. She had identified that while the use of the 'Suffolk Grids' (available for download at www.sandgateprimary.co.uk/tracking/levelling.htm), was a good tool for her to use to assess pupils' progress, and supported her in using 'Closing the Gap' marking, she was concerned that the most able writers were not achieving their full potential. This was often due to poor punctuation, or a lack of topic-specific vocabulary being used. Sandeep also felt that the children did not have sufficient time to reflect on their writing – or even read it again fully! She wanted to ensure that the children had the opportunity to reflect on their own work, and understand what they could do to improve their next piece of non-narrative writing.

Sandeep developed a 'child-friendly' version of the 'Suffolk Grids' (see Figure 6.1), and allowed children to read their work, and highlight the statements that they felt they had achieved.

Once the children had done this, they exchanged work with a partner, discussed it and highlighted the grid together, checking that they both agreed with the highlighted statements. Sandeep then gave the children the 'levels' that matched each column on the grid (this had not been presented to them in the first instance, as the trainee did not want the level to influence which column the children highlighted). Children then used a reflection sheet (Figure 6.2) to help them to identify the strengths and weaknesses of their work, and specifically what they would need to do on their next piece of work.

Sandeep commented that children were genuinely surprised that they had missed out important punctuation, or hadn't included topic-specific vocabulary. Prior to the next non-narrative writing task, she recapped on the improvements that the children had suggested for themselves, and revisited their reflection sheets. All the children involved in the self/peer-assessment grids and reflection sheets improved their non-narrative writing by at least one-third of a level (3a to 4c), with one child improving two-thirds of a level (3b to 4c). Children also noted that they found the reflection sheet and grids helpful in identifying improvements for their own writing. Children were engaged in improving their own learning and the assessment tasks provided them with a sense of responsibility and achievement.

Sandeep aims to plan more time for self- and peer-assessment within her classroom. She feels that meaningful self/peer-assessment should have a place within every classroom, rather than what she describes as the tokenistic 'thumbs up, thumbs down' form of self-assessment. She now aims to target other underachieving writers, in order to help them to achieve to their full potential. The trainee stated that giving children responsibility for making improvements to their own learning empowered them and they also appeared to be a lot keener to participate in writing activities.

Non-Narrative Self-Assessment Sheet: 3b   3a   4c

Features	I think that my writing... (3b)	I think that my writing... (3a)	I think that my writing... (4c)
Structure and organisation of your writing	1. Has different sections (containing different information) are separate. 2. Keeps information about the same subject in the same sections.	1. Has a clear introduction and conclusion. 2. Has the correct and layout – numbering OR line breaks OR paragraphs.	1. Has a clear introduction and conclusion. 2. Has sections written in order. 3. Has each new section clearly indicated. 4. Shows that my ideas presented clearly.
Writing for an audience	3. Uses language that interests the reader. 4. Uses language that provides details.	3. Shows the same viewpoint most of the way through.	5. Shows the same viewpoint all the way through. 6. Uses details to try to interest the reader.
Using language effectively	5. Sometimes includes language that creates effects. 6. Includes simple noun phrases. 7. Includes a great range of vocabulary.	4. Regularly includes language that creates effects. 5. Includes expanded noun phrases. 6. Includes some adverbial phrases.	7. Includes expanded noun phrases. 8. Includes adverbial phrases. 9. Includes technical OR topic specific vocabulary.
Sentence construction	8. Includes simple sentences. 9. Includes compound sentences with simple connectives. 10. Sometimes includes pronouns. 11. Includes a variety of sentence openings.	7. Includes simple sentences. 8. Includes compound sentences with lots of different connectives. 9. Includes a variety of sentence openings which highlight my main ideas.	10. Uses complex sentences to add extra information.
Punctuation	12. Is mostly punctuated well, with full stops and capital letters. 13. Sometimes includes question marks and exclamation marks.	10. Is mostly punctuated well, with full stops, capital letters, question marks and exclamation marks. 11. Inverted commas are used when speech starts and finishes.	11. Is mostly punctuated well, with full stops, capital letters, question marks and exclamation marks. 12. Includes commas within my lists. 13. Includes the use of apostrophes for omission.

Figure 6.1: Example of a child's self-assessment

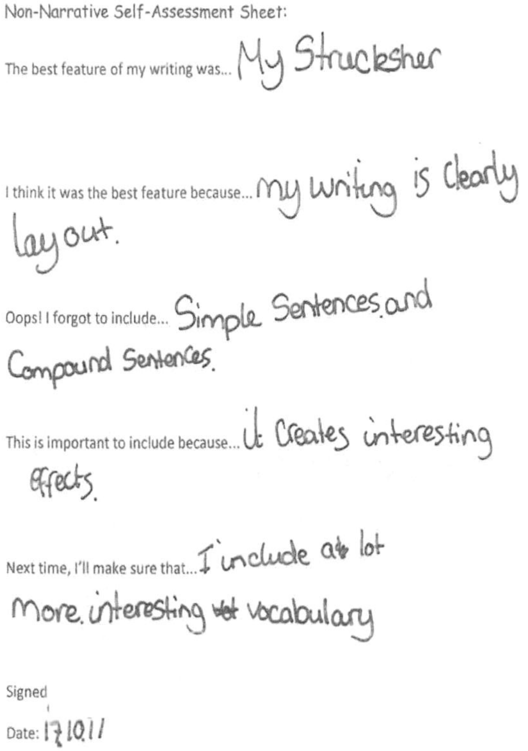

Non-Narrative Self-Assessment Sheet:

The best feature of my writing was... *My Strucksher*

I think it was the best feature because... *my writing is clearly layout.*

Oops! I forgot to include... *Simple Sentences and Compound Sentences.*

This is important to include because... *It creates interesting effects.*

Next time, I'll make sure that... *I include a lot more interesting vocabulary*

Signed

Date: *17.10.11*

Figure 6.2: Example of a child's reflection sheet

Activity

Plan a self-assessment episode. What strategies are you going to use? Why? How will you prepare children for this? How do you plan to use the assessment information in future work?

Pupil peer-assessment

A key advantage of peer-assessment is that it can contribute to children's personal and social development. Peer-assessment allows opportunities for children to understand how to communicate with each other, how to provide sensitive, constructive feedback and for each to develop a shared understanding of learning. Through considering each other's work, children can gain a clearer understanding of what is expected, and can identify strengths and areas for development in their own work. The notion of peers working collaboratively is not revolutionary and there is a significant body of knowledge regarding the topics of collaborative learning and group work. Corden (2000) draws on a range of studies to highlight the potential for cognitive and social development through peer collaboration. However, what is of interest, and pertinent to this chapter, is that in organising and managing collaborative learning there is research to demonstrate that it will not simply happen merely because a teacher has sat children together and given them an instruction.

The implication, therefore, is that for peer-assessment to be successful, children need to understand why they are being asked to work collaboratively and see the relevance of and recognise what it means to be working in such a manner.

Activity

How would you manage peer-assessment? Does it just happen? Do you plan for it? Has this always been successful? What challenges have you experienced?

Using self-assessment to improve your academic achievement

The above sections have focused on self- and peer-assessment from a classroom-based perspective. However, while self- and peer-assessment strategies are valuable learning and teaching tools in the primary classroom, there are opportunities, as you develop as an academic writer and as a practitioner, for you to engage in self- and peer-assessment.

Often in higher education institutes there is great emphasis placed on summative assessment, and arguably many students have few opportunities to engage in self- and peer- assessment. The locus of control with regard to assessment, and feedback in particular, lies with tutors.

However, if one reflects on the research evidence related to the potential impact of involving children in the assessment and feedback process, this seems somewhat out of step with current thoughts about formative assessment in primary education.

Research Focus

Feedback, Orsmond, Merry and Reiling (2002) claim, is inseparable from the learning process, with successful students making prudent use of tutors' feedback. Yet, while this is commendable, Wotjas (1998) reported on the research findings in one university, suggesting that some students were concerned only with their mark and not with the feedback. This is endorsed by Duncan (2007), who notes that many students from his own institution show little interest in the written or oral advice offered to them by the markers.

Activity

Do you always collect your assessment feedback? Do you read it? What do you do with it? How could you make good use of assessment feedback to impact on future achievements?

Given that tutors spend large amounts of time in providing students with feedback, the issues raised in the research are concerning. In efforts to help students engage more fully with feedback and to begin to engage in self-assessment, we have introduced a number of initiatives at my institution. The first, which should be of interest to you, is very practical. We ask that students maintain a 'feedback folder', and on receipt of feedback they complete a self-assessment target sheet (see Appendix 2). Students and tutors alike have commented very favourably about these.

Activity
Complete a self-assessment target sheet (Appendix 2). Track your progress and identify future targets.

Using self-assessment to improve your teaching

In addition to using self-assessment strategies to impact on academic achievement, self-assessment can prove to be a useful technique for improving classroom practice. The pro forma (Appendix 2) can be adapted to focus on classroom-based practice. In efforts to support trainees with regard to self-assessment, not only do they complete the pro forma, they also engage in deep analysis of their practice. Trainees I work with are asked to identify three pedagogical targets for development during their final assessed school-based placement. They reflect on their prior experiences and theory in order to fully assess a specific aspect of teaching and learning. To illuminate this for you, the following case study presents excerpts from Sharron's work.

Case Study: Sharron's reflection

The following extract is included with permission from the trainee.

Target: To include children in the self-assessment process

As Wiliam et al. (2010) discovered, substantial learning gains are possible when teachers introduce formative assessment into their classrooms, particularly developing strategies that children can use to improve their own learning such as target-setting. On developmental placement I used a variety of methods to collect children's self-assessments relating to tasks, including strategies such as smiley faces, traffic lights and thumbs up, thumbs down in plenary sessions. My placement Report form B identified that I could further enhance my knowledge of self-assessment strategies and use other ways of gathering

$\rightarrow$

assessment involving children's own perceptions of their learning. This target will discuss the underpinning theory and explore why self-assessment and target-setting is a very important skill for children to acquire. Furthermore, it will discuss how involving children in their self-assessment and target-setting can help raise achievement through increased self-esteem.

Planning, teaching and assessment are all part of a cyclical process (Jones, 2009) and are fundamental to the learning process within the classroom. Black and Wiliam (1998) consider self-assessment as a critical skill to be developed by learners within the classroom because it gives children a central role in learning, helping them develop the necessary critical skills such as self-evaluation needed for life-long learning. Zimmerman (2001) acknowledges that students' perceptions of themselves as learners and the use of various processes to regulate their learning are critical factors in analyses of academic achievement. Similarly, Pritchard (2009), Dann (2002) and Harrison and Howard (2009) agree that in order to take learning forward, children need to take responsibility for their learning and work collaboratively with teachers and peers to further enhance the learning process, rather than simply being passive recipients in the learning process.

However, although this raises a critical point about self-assessment, it would be naive to assume that pupils will simply be able to understand the complexities of self-assessment and be suitably equipped to judge the next steps in their learning. Hence, as Black and Wiliam (1998), Raiker (2007) and Wallace (2001) discuss, children need to be guided and taught to self-assess and target-set correctly, otherwise they may misjudge their level of achievement. Thus, when developing targets with children I will need to provide opportunities for discussion and reflection and scaffold children appropriately in the process of self-assessment. Clarke (2001) acknowledges that if children learn the ability to self-assess through ipsative referencing, which involves setting targets measured against previous attainment, self-esteem improves. As Shetton and Bromhill (2008) and Schunk (2001) acknowledge, if children are able to see progress in their own learning then in turn their intrinsic motivation and self-esteem will be improved. However, although there is clear evidence that involving children in self-assessment and target-setting is beneficial, Clarke (2001) warns that if teachers are too generous with the targets they can be reached too easily, resulting in a high turnover of targets and an unmanageable assessment system. On the contrary, it could also be argued that if teachers overestimate the capabilities of children and set targets that are too hard to reach, a negative effect on the child's self-esteem will occur when they fail to reach the criteria set within the target (Ross et al, 2008). Therefore, I must ensure I undertake careful consideration of children's strengths and capabilities when setting targets for children to assess themselves against within my classroom.

→

As highlighted through the discussion above, target-setting and involving children in the self-assessment process is clearly beneficial in helping children develop an awareness of themselves and in helping them to identify their strengths and weaknesses in different aspects of the curriculum. However, there needs to be opportunities for learners to be able to discuss and reflect on their learning if self-assessment is to be beneficial in moving learning forward. Similarly, I must be careful to ensure on placement that I involve children in the target-setting process and clearly identify targets for future development, sharing these in a way children can understand in relation to the set learning outcomes. I look forward to developing and implementing this on my forthcoming synoptic placement.

Activity

Sharron has reflected on her experiences in the classroom and on a range of literature to assess the importance of pupil self-assessment. To what extent do you reflect on theoretical perspectives to make judgements about practice and to assess your teaching? Do you think it is important to do this? Why?

In addition to self-assessment, the role of peer-assessment in higher education is an important teaching and learning strategy.

Using peer-assessment to improve your academic writing

Research Focus

Peer-assessment, Davies (2006), Morris (2001) and Orsmond (2006) claim, serves as a metacognitive assessment tool which engages students in the development of their own learning. According to Janes (2007), peer-assessment can be effective in deepening students' learning, development and reflection of subject-related content while concurrently gaining an appreciation of academic conventions and technicalities. Such assertions are supported by others in the field. For example, research by Ballantyne, Hughes and Mylonas (2002) notes that students commonly report that assessing their own or their peers' work can be personally motivating; they develop knowledge and understanding of subject content and it helps with their learning, and also with understanding the assessment process more fully.

The process of peer-assessment requires students to closely examine their peers' work, guided by assessment criteria. This activity, Vu and Dall'Alba (2007) notes, helps students to diversify their own approaches and strategies in undertaking a learning task and can deepen understanding about high- or low-quality

$\rightarrow$

performance (Gibbs 1999, McDowell and Sambell 1999). Thus students can better understand their own learning and the feedback they receive from assessment.

Nevertheless, there are potential pitfalls associated with peer-assessment that are acknowledged in the literature. For example, the use of peer-assessment may result in increased time and workload for both teachers and students, as time is devoted to preparing students for the process. If peer-assessment is introduced purely as a supplementary activity for feedback, the additional time and workload involved may result in its being unpopular with teachers and students alike (Farmer and Eastcott, 1995).

Secondly, Williams (1992), for example, reported that although students in her study found peer-assessment interesting, some felt uncomfortable doing it as they saw it as a form of criticism of their friends.

One means of supporting trainees with the peer-assessment process is to ensure that, as with children, they are very clear of the purpose of the exercise.

Case Study: Being a critical friend

Trainees who were moving from Year 1 to Year 2 of a BA (Honours) Primary Undergraduate Programme were encouraged, during the summer vacation, to prepare the first part of a three-part assignment designed to develop their subject specialism of Personal Social, Health and Citizenship Education (PSHCE). This required that trainees submit a 500-word reflection on what and how they have learned in relation to their previous experience of PSHCE. On their return to university (week 1) trainees were advised that they would be encouraged to complete a peer-review exercise of the draft assignment in week 3. In the session, the tutor focused the discussion around the following:

What makes a critical friend?

- Someone with whom you can discuss issues and seek constructive advice from.

- Someone with whom a relationship should be good and whose opinion you value.

- Someone to whom you can give critical advice.

- The relationship should be treated as a commitment and a responsibility.

The tutor stated that it was highly important, as part of the peer-review process, that the trainees not only knew why the peer-review activity was important to developing their skills in reflective writing, but also what their role would be. The trainees commented as follows:

By assessing someone else's work, I was also able to pick up on my own mistakes. I think it did improve my work because I took on board my colleague's comments and made the appropriate adjustments.

$\rightarrow$

I found this to be a very positive process. The comments given to me allowed me to reflect on my work and subsequently change it to become, what I feel, a better piece of work. It allowed my colleague and myself the opportunity to discuss the topic, helping us to think about different ways of explaining and writing. I would like it if we could do this more.

I found the peer-review task very effective. It allowed me to gain positive and constructive feedback and I was able to understand the question more clearly and it enabled me to reflect on my understanding of the set task.

While the majority of trainees were highly positive about the experience, some trainees commented that they still found it challenging to give feedback to a 'friend'.

Activity

How often have you engaged in peer-assessment as part of your studies? How do you feel about it? Think about how you manage children's peer-assessment opportunities. It is important to reflect on how *you* feel as a learner in a peer-assessment context so that you can engage with children more effectively.

Reducing the discomfort associated with peer-assessment may be mitigated against through using anonymised pieces of work.

Case Study

In the final year of their degree programme, trainees are asked to set three pedagogical targets for their final placement, as outlined earlier in the chapter. Having decided on these, they are required to conduct research on each target and to submit an academic piece of work. Ensuring targets are clear and focused is key to this assessment. To support trainees with this, they are given the assessment information in advance of the summer vacation, and advised to draft a target and begin to conduct research. In addition, a trainee who had successfully completed the programme consented to her assignment being used to support future trainees. The trainees were therefore given a 'snapshot' of a completed assignment, during the summer vacation, and asked to respond to the following:

1. Read the 'snapshot' of the assignment.

2. Note initial thoughts about the work – to what extent does it meet the assessment criteria?

3. What 'grade' do you think this achieved?

4. What advice would you give to the reader?

5. What have you learned about yourself as a writer from reading this?

6. What advice will you now give to yourself?

→

> The trainees completed this activity independently in the first instance, and then shared their responses in pairs and small groups when in taught sessions. They were then guided by a tutor and moved to begin to critique their own draft assignments.
>
> The trainees commented that the use of a model brought to life the assessment expectations, made them aware of what they needed to do well, and made the grading criteria explicit.

Activity

Do you have the opportunity to 'see' models? What benefits and/or challenges could this present? Would you share models with children in your classrooms? Why?

Using peer-assessment to improve school-based training

The traditional model of initial teacher training has tended to adopt an individualistic approach, whereby individual trainees undertake solo placements within individual classes. However, while there are merits to developing as an autonomous teacher within the classroom, this model has been subject to criticism (Bullough et al, 2002) and research in the field has acknowledged that with the increasing emphasis on teaching as a collaborative venture, trainee teachers need to be prepared for this. One means of facilitating this is through providing opportunities for 'paired placements'.

Paired (or small group) placements promote opportunities for two or more trainee teachers to work collaboratively with a class teacher and peer(s) such that they can engage in peer-learning and peer-assessment. With regard to peer-learning, the rationale for paired placements is that a 'two-way reciprocal learning activity' can take place (Boud, 2001, p.3) as it allows for the trainees to plan lessons, prepare resources, teach and assess collaboratively. With regard to peer-assessment, paired placements allow trainees to engage in joint observation of each other's lessons and the class teacher's lesson, followed, perhaps, by a collaborative three-way discussion including the class teacher.

Supporting trainee teachers during paired placements is key, and at our institution we have opportunities for trainees to work in pairs during their very first placement. We are aware that for many of our trainee teachers, the first placement can be a daunting experience and we believe that, as Bullough et al (2002, p.74) report, students who have experienced paired placements provided 'emotional support to one another, [and] they became interested in and invested in one another's successes'.

To support trainees during their initial placement, clear tasks are provided to ensure trainees are working collaboratively in undertaking self- and peer-assessment.

Case Study: Peer- and self-assessment on placement

Task outline

- With your partner, you are going to plan and implement an exploratory or investigative science activity with the whole class, using your class teacher's plans and using him/her for support during the planning and implementation of the lesson.

- You and your partner will then implement the plan with the whole class. You will share responsibility for the introduction to everyone and the conclusion/plenary. You will then work with the class and you may plan for your class teacher to support some of the children in the exploratory or investigative stages of the session.

- If there is time while you are carrying out the activity, try to note down any points of interest that arise as the activity develops, such as children's comments or actions, questions raised.

Reflection points
- Evaluate your shared planning and implementation, ensuring consideration of the following aspects:
  - The introduction, development and conclusion
  - Interest levels
  - Use of active learning
  - Children's role
  - Teacher's role

- What indications did you gain of the children's achievements? Were there any significant differences in ideas or use of process skills between individual children?

Activity

What do you think are the advantages of peer-learning and assessment during school-based training? How do you feel about giving feedback to a peer on placement? How do you feel about receiving feedback from a peer?

Other opportunities for peer-assessment can be afforded through the use of video. Recent work conducted at Stranmillis University College, presented at a Teacher Education conference, highlighted the possibility of using video clips of trainee teachers, recorded during their first teaching episode, to support reflection and self- and peer-assessment (see http://cumbria.ac.uk/AboutUs/Subjects/Education/Research/TEAN/TeacherEducatorsStorehouse/TEANConference2011.aspx). Adrian Copping also discusses the use of video in Chapter 3.

Activity

What advantages are there to videoing practice and allowing others to comment on this? What are the disadvantages? How would you feel?

Learning Outcomes Review

In this chapter you have explored the difference between assessment and evaluation, and been encouraged to plan a range of self- and peer-assessment opportunities. The chapter has also identified the importance of reflecting on your own practice, including considering theoretical perspectives, to improve teaching and learning.

Self-assessment questions

1. Why and how would you plan for self/peer-assessment opportunities in your classroom?
2. What strategies could you employ in your classroom to help you to reflect on your practice?
3. What opportunities do you have for collaborative teaching?

Further reading

Clarke, S. (2008) *Active Learning Through Formative Assessment*. London: Hodder Education. For practical suggestions and ideas about self- and peer-assessment.

The Campaign for Learning website has a range of case studies from the learning to learn project, and there are practical examples of teachers implementing self- and peer-assessment strategies included: www.campaignforlearning.org.uk/cfl/learninginschools/l2l/index.asp

Gardner, J. (2006) *Assessment and Learning*. London: SAGE.

For further information about assessment more broadly:

Swaffield, S. (2008) *Unlocking Assessment: Understanding for reflection and application*. London: Routledge.

References

Ballantyne, R., Hughes, K. and Mylonas, A. (2002) Developing Procedures for Implementing Peer Assessment in Large Classes Using an Action Research Process. *Assessment and Evaluation in Higher Education*, 27(5): 427–41.

Black, P. and Wiliam, D. (1998) *Inside the Black Box: Raising Standards through Classroom Assessment*. London: King's College.

Bloom, B.S., Hastings, J.T. and Maddaus, G.F. (1971) *Handbook on Formative and Summative Evaluation of Student Learning.* New York: McGraw-Hill.

Boud, D. (2001) Introduction: Making the move to peer learning. In D. Boud, R. Cohen and J. Sampson (eds) *Peer Learning in Higher Education: Learning From and With Each Other.* London: Kogan Page.

Bullough, R.V., Young, J., Erickson, L., Birrell, J.R., Clark, C., Egan, M.W., Berrie, C. F., Hales, V. and Smith, G. (2002) Rethinking field experiences: partnership teaching versus single-placement teaching. *Journal of Teacher Education,* 53(1): 68–80.

Clarke, S. (2001) *Unlocking Formative Assessment: Practical Strategies for Enhancing Pupils' Learning in the Primary Classroom.* London: Hodder & Stoughton Education.

Corden, R. (2000) *Literacy and Learning through Talk: Strategies for the Primary Classroom.* Buckingham: Open University Press.

Dann, R. (2002) *Promoting Assessment as Learning: Improving the Learning Process.* London: RoutledgeFalmer.

Davies, P. (2006) Peer assessment: Judging the quality of students' work by comments rather than marks. *Innovations in Education and Teaching International,* 43(1): 69.

Duncan, N. (2007) 'Feed-forward': improving students' use of tutors' comments. *Assessment and Evaluation in Higher Education,* 32(3): 271–83.

Farmer, B. and Eastcott, D. (1995) Making assessment a positive experience. In P. Knight, (ed) *Assessment for Learning in Higher Education.* London: Kogan Page.

Gibbs, G. (1999) Using assessment strategically to change the way students learn. In S. Brown and A. Glasner (eds) *Assessment Matters in Higher Education: Choosing and Using Diverse Approaches.* Buckingham: Open University Press.

Gipps, C.V. and Murphy, P. (1994) *A Fair Test? Assessment, Achievement and Equity.* Buckingham and Philadelphia: Open University Press.

Gipps, C. (1994) *Beyond Testing: Towards a Theory of Educational Assessment.* London: Falmer Press.

Harlen, W. (1994) *Enhancing Quality in Assessment.* London: Paul Chapman.

Harrison, C. and Howard, S. (2009) *Inside the Primary Black Box: Assessment for Learning in Primary and Early Years Classrooms.* London: GL Assessment.

Janes, D. (2007). Self, peer and group assessment in e-learning. *British Journal of Educational Technology,* 38(1): 175–6.

Jones, D. (2009) Speaking and listening: planning assessment. In D. Jones and P. Hodson (eds) *Unlocking Speaking and Listening.* Oxon: Routledge.

McDowell, L. and Sambell, K (1999) Fitness for purpose in the assessment of student learning: students as stakeholders. *Quality in Higher Education*, 5(2): 107–23.

Morris, J. (2001), Peer assessment: A missing link between teaching and learning? A Review of the Literature, *Nurse Education Today*, October.

Orsmond, P. (2006) *Self- and Peer-assessment: Guidance on Practice in the Biosciences*, Higher Education Academy.

Orsmond, P., Merry, S. and Reiling, K. (2002) Assessment and Evaluation in Higher Education 27: 309–23. The use of examplars and formative feedback when using student derived marking criteria in peer and self-assessment.

Pritchard, A. (2009) *Ways of Learning: Learning Theories and Learning Styles in the Classroom.* 2nd ed. Oxon: Routledge.

Raiker, A. (2007) Assessment for learning. In K. Jacques and R. Hyland *Professional Studies: Primary and Early Years.* Exeter: Learning Matters.

Ross, P., Little, E. and Keinhuis, M. (2008) Self-reported and actual use of proactive and reactive classroom management strategies and their relationship with teacher stress and student behaviour. *Educational Psychology,* 28(6): 693–710 (www.swetswise.com, accessed 21/10/11).

Schunk, D.H. (2001) Social cognitive theory and self-regulated learning. In B.J. Zimmerman and D.H. Schunk (eds) *Self-Regulated Learning and Academic Achievement: Theoretical Perspectives.* Mahwah NJ: Lawrence Elbaum Associates (www.netlibrary.com, accessed 17/10/11).

Shetton, F. and Bromhill, S. (2008) *Effective Behaviour Management in the Primary Classroom.* Berkshire: Open University Press.

Torrance, H. and Pryor, J. (1998) *Investigating Formative Assessment: Teaching and Learning in the Classroom.* Guildford: Biddles Ltd.

Tunstall, P. and Gipps, C. (1996) Teacher feedback to young children in formative assessment: a typology. *Curriculum Journal,* 22(4): 206–24.

Vu, T. T. and Dall'Alba G. (2007) Students' experience of peer-assessment in a professional course. *Assessment and Evaluation in Higher Education,* 32(5): 541–56.

Wallace, B. (2001) So what's new about teaching children to think?' In B. Wallace (ed) *Teaching Thinking Skills Across the Primary Curriculum.* London: David Fulton.

Wiliam, D., Lee, C., Harrison, C. and Black, P. (2010) Teachers developing assessment for learning: Impact on student achievement. *Assessment in Education: Principles, Policy and Practice Quarterly.* 11(1): 48–66 (www.swetswise.com, accessed 21/1011).

Williams, E. (1992). Student attitudes towards approaches to learning and assessment. *Assessment and Evaluation in Higher Education,* 17: 45–58.

Wotjas, O. (1998) Feedback? No, just give us the answers. *Times Higher Education Supplement*, 25 September.

Zimmerman, B.J. (2001) Theories of self-regulated learning and academic achievement: An overview and analysis. In D.H. Schunk and B.J. Zimmerman *Self-Regulated Learning and Academic Achievement: Theoretical Perspectives.* Mahwah, NJ: Lawrence Erlbaum Associates (www.netlibrary.com, accessed 17/1011).

7. Reflection through Lesson Study
Pete Dudley and Elizabeth Gowing

Learning Outcomes

By the end of this chapter you will have learned:

- about Lesson Study and how to carry it out in school-based professional learning contexts and also those of initial teacher training;
- how to use case illustrations of Lesson Study as triggers to plan your own approach;
- how to reflect upon your experience and plan approaches to sharing what you have learned and developed with others.

Reflective practice

This chapter takes a look at professional learning through Lesson Study from a socio-cultural perspective (see Research Focus below). However, Lesson Study can also be seen as a form of highly orchestrated reflective practice. Despite pre-dating the literature which developed the idea of reflective practice, Lesson Study (LS) is nevertheless a very distinct form of reflective and *reflexive* practice. Reflective practice is the capacity to reflect on action so as to engage in a process of continuous learning and is identified by Schön as one of the defining characteristics of professional practice (Schön, 1983). Lesson Study is *reflective* because groups of teachers repeatedly reflect upon evidence they have gathered about their pupils, their curriculum, their lessons, the way their pupils are learning and their pupils' views about all this. It is *reflexive* because as teachers review the way their pupils have learned in sequences of collectively planned 'research lessons', they adjust their understanding of their pupils' learning and in turn adjust their subsequent teaching.

Research Focus

The research focus for this chapter is on how children learn and how their teachers learn. It draws upon research in areas of learning, teaching, teacher learning and practice transfer.

Socio-cultural theory

Socio-cultural theory has become a dominant lens that helps us to understand how people learn. Socio-cultural theorists have focused on how people utilise talk in learning – on how language and interaction are the means through which we learn.

$\rightarrow$

The architect of socio-cultural theory is Vygotsky (1986), who first suggested that thought and language are inextricably linked. One cannot exist without the other. He claims that we learn through interacting with others (for example as babies first learning to talk and interact with adults and siblings) and later through interacting – with others through talk and with ourselves through articulating thoughts and listening to them through the 'voice' in our heads with which we articulate much of our thinking to ourselves and develop our ideas and concepts. There is more about Vygotsky's theories of language and learning, and their particular application in teaching, in the General Teaching Council for England's materials on Vygotsky which is part of their Research for Teachers series (available through: www.canterbury.ac.uk/).

Effective professional learning

Understanding the elements of Lesson Study and the reason they are effective for professional learning draws on research into teacher knowledge and professional learning. The most comprehensive review of the elements that make for successful teacher learning was carried out by the EPPI Centre into the impact of collaborative CPD (Cordingley et al, 2003). This systematic review of research identified the following features as essential ingredients of professional development which has an impact on classroom teaching and learning:

- Observation with professional dialogue
- The use of external expertise linked to in-school activity
- Peer support
- Scope for teacher participants to identify their own professional learning focus
- Processes to encourage, extend and structure professional dialogue
- Sustaining the professional learning over time

Activity
Reflect on something new you have learned successfully in your professional life. What led to you learning it so effectively? Did it share any of the features of effective professional development above? If not, what else made it such a successful learning experience for you?

Pupil voice

A body of work that has developed considerably in the past 15 years in England (e.g. Macintyre et al, 2007; Rudduck and Flutter, 2010) focuses on the legitimate involvement of the perspectives, voices and action of children in the processes of teaching and learning and in reflecting upon practice themselves. This pupil perspective is an essential component of the Lesson Study approach to professional learning. Experience shows that the insights of pupils, expressed with a child's directness rather than the careful diplomacy of adults, is feedback that is likely to change practice.

What is Lesson Study

Lesson Study (LS) has been in use by Japanese teachers since the 1870s. It is therefore older than western concepts such as reflective practice, and even action research, which dates back to the Second World War. LS is a form of collaborative continuing professional learning practised by groups of Japanese teachers and school leaders throughout their careers. At any point in his or her career, a Japanese teacher is likely to be a member of at least one Lesson Study group.

In fact LS is only the educational version of a form of collective problem-solving that exists across many facets of life in Japan, including business and industry (Dudley, 2011a). In order to improve the efficiency of, for example, a particular car component, a frequently employed practice in the Japanese motor industry is to take a cross-section of people who have different perspectives on the particular model of car – perhaps one or two people involved in production of the car, a designer, someone who drives one of these cars, maybe even one of the company directors. These people then pool their knowledge and expertise and work together on making the component even more reliable and effective. For this to work the members of the group observe a protocol based on a spirit of openness, equality and commitment to learning and joint enquiry. Thus, as they work together on solving the problem, all group members are of equal status and everyone is treated with respect.

As we shall argue later in this chapter, this equality of status and joint ownership of the problem and the jointly discovered solution is profoundly important when it comes to teacher learning – whether the teacher is experienced, newly qualified or in initial training.

How Lesson Study works

In Lesson Study groups of teachers who want to improve an aspect of pupil learning in their school or department come together as equals, committed to learning together through collaborative enquiry. Much of this enquiry takes place in classroom lessons. They do this in order to improve practice and to develop new aspects of their practice knowledge. The process of conducting a lesson study involved the following stages repeated in three or more 'Lesson Study cycles' (see Figure 7.1).

1. Identifying a focus.
2. Identifying case pupils.
3. Planning a research lesson.
4. Conducting the research lesson and gathering evidence of the pupils' learning – particularly the case pupils.

5. Interviewing case pupils (and sometimes other pupils) about the research lesson.

6. Conducting a post-lesson discussion to review the pupils' learning and to begin to identify points for the next research lesson.

7. Passing on to others what has been learned by the Lesson Study group and capturing this on record.

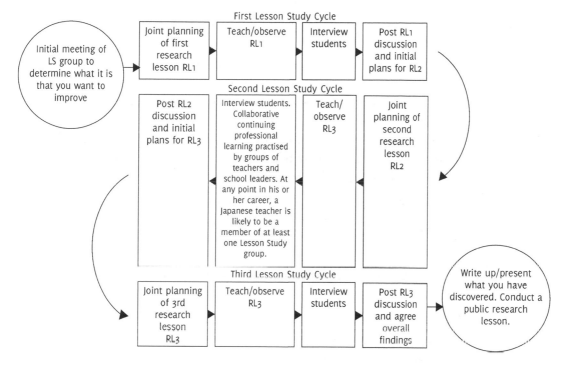

© Bethlehem University: Lesson Study Toolkit (Dudley, 2011b)

Figure 7.1. A three cycle lesson study

1. The teachers involved identify an aspect of teaching that needs to be improved. They find out what research suggests approaches that are worth pursuing in order to improve the learning of the particular kinds of pupils they are focusing on in the curriculum areas that they are going to teach and they decide on an approach to try out and develop.

2. As the teachers are planning they often focus on a small number of specific children who may typify learner groups within the class (higher, middle or lower attaining, for example) or, alternatively, who may represent the kinds of pupils whose learning they are trying to improve (less-engaged boys, for example). These are called 'case pupils'.

3. They plan the research lesson carefully with these specific pupils in mind, aiming to make the research lesson work for each of these pupils at each stage of the lesson by spelling out *exactly* what they expect these pupils to be doing and learning at each of these stages. This requires the group to be very, very clear about the intended outcomes of the lesson for each

of these pupils. It also requires the group to be very clear and agreed about the specific learning needs of these pupils. As a result, the Lesson Study group members become accountable to each other at a very detailed level of the lesson plan. If any member of the LS group misunderstands an aspect of the lesson that is being planned, it becomes clear very quickly and the group cannot move forward until the issue is resolved.

4. Having planned it, the LS group then conducts their 'research lesson' in which one member of the group will teach the lesson while the rest observe and make notes – paying particular but not exclusive attention to the learning of the three or four case pupils.

5. Immediately after the research lesson they interview children (often the case pupils) about their experience in the research lesson – asking them about the way the lesson had worked, how the techniques they employed had affected the pupils' learning and how a similar lesson could be improved another time for similar pupils. These pupils may even be involved in the subsequent planning processes. In some schools, where the age and ability of the pupils permits it, the pupils are all given a written questionnaire, which might then be followed up with a sample of pupils for interview.

6. The teachers then conduct a post-lesson discussion that examines the learning of each of the pupils, comparing what the group had planned that the pupil would do and learn with what actually happened in the research lesson – and then seeking to explain any differences. This sequence of discussion is of critical importance to the LS process because it keeps the teachers' focus on the learning and not (at this stage) on the teaching. This helps to preserve the sense of joint ownership of the research lesson and the group's willingness to take risks and learn from what has not gone according to plan as well as what has (see Figure 7.2).

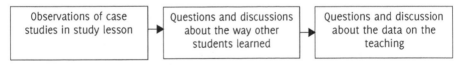

Reproduced with permission from *Lesson Study: A Handbook* (Dudley, 2011c)

Figure 7.2: Post-lesson discussion sequence

This whole process is likely to be repeated three or four times as the teachers tweak, adjust and refine the approach that they are developing in each research lesson until they believe that they have isolated and perfected an aspect of practice that could be used by other teachers. This marks the completion of a 'Lesson Study cycle'.

7. A very important part of the process involves members of the Lesson Study group passing on their new knowledge to other professionals. In Japan they may invite colleagues to their school and carry out a lesson where the new approach is used and observed by their guests who are invited into the classroom to watch. This is called an 'open house'. Alternatively, they may stage a demonstration of the approach in the hall after school in front of a larger audience. This is a 'public research lesson'. In both cases the approach, once demonstrated, is discussed with members of the audience by the teachers (and often the children as well).

Activity

If you were to embark on a cycle of Lesson Study next week, what would your chosen focus be? Consider an area of your practice that you would like to know more about, where you feel you are not as successful as in other areas or where you are baffled by your pupils' response.

Who would your 'case pupils' be? They should be children representative of groups in the class and/or those whose learning you are particularly interested in this area. Identifying these children may in itself be an important step in scrutinising what is going on in the teaching and learning of your class.

Case study

Kerry and Emina are trainee teachers in the same school. Kerry's placement is in Year 3 and Emina's in Year 6. The two wanted to work together and tried doing peer observations in each other's classes but they found that it was hard to find points of overlap in their different contexts. Emina thinks that Kerry's effective behaviour management systems in Year 3 would be seen as 'too babyish' in Year 6, and what Kerry admired about the way that Emina's Year 6 pupils worked independently in groups seemed too difficult to transfer to her younger children working on a very different curriculum. They have both asked for feedback from their school-based mentor, a friendly teacher whose classroom they both admire. When she came to do observations of their lessons they both took care to do lessons they knew would be successful – Kerry didn't risk doing group work, and Emina stuck to the activities where she knew her children would excel and be focused. As a result they have very positive evaluations from their mentor, but are still feeling that they would like to improve their teaching.

They decided to start a Lesson Study together. After discussion they identified that the common challenge they were experiencing in their teaching, making both behaviour management and effective group work difficult, were groups of able and sometimes arrogant children. In Emina's Year 6 a group of boys were dismissive of the work they were set, saying it was too easy, and this was sometimes the starting point for off-task and disruptive behaviour, and in Kelly's Year 3 class there was a similar group of girls and boys who worked very assiduously when on their own, but didn't like to be 'slowed down' by working with less able pupils when she set up group work activities. They decided to start by planning a lesson to be taught in Emina's Year 6 class, designed to address the needs of these more able pupils and give them enough interesting challenge that they would stay on-task. When they started planning they weren't sure whether it would be Emina or Kerry who would actually teach the lesson.

They thought together about what the features were of lessons where their challenging groups of pupils did best, and identified that these pupils seemed to

$\rightarrow$

perform better both in groups and on their own when they were able to contribute to designing the challenge in their learning, and evaluating how well they met their self-designated target. They therefore constructed an activity where the class was asked individually and then in groups to come up with their own success criteria for a music task. At points through the lesson the groups were to be asked to evaluate their progress against their identified success criteria on a tick sheet.

Having combined their ideas to write the plan, they decided at the end who would actually teach the lesson, and then arranged for Emina to come and watch Kerry's lesson, keeping in front of her all the time the plan where they had noted very carefully exactly what they hoped Ian, Jordan, Betim and Daniel would be doing at each stage. As she watched she noted interesting responses and where the boys were responding as they had hoped, and where there were surprises.

After the lesson Emina and Kerry together interviewed the four boys and asked what they thought about the lesson, what they had learned, and what had helped them. The boys said they liked having had the self-designated criteria for success, and Daniel even commented, 'We should have one of those in maths too.'

The trainee teachers then looked over the plans in the light of what they had noted themselves in the lesson, and what the boys had fed back to them. Their new approach seemed to have had a positive impact on the quality of group work, so they planned to try a similar thing in the Year 3 class the following week, in the second Lesson Study cycle. If it was successful there too then they would ask to share it with others in their university study group at the next tutor meeting.

Why Lesson Study works

In the process of planning together...

The Lesson Study process encourages teachers to take risks as a group and become increasingly absorbed in improving learning for identified learners. The planning group makes manifest the detail of the learning and teaching that they are planning by 'rehearsing' and re-rehearsing many aspects of their research lessons in role as teachers in order to draw upon their tacit knowledge of the classroom and teaching and to make it visible to others in the group (Dudley, 2010). This process allows teachers to question and reconfigure deeply held beliefs about teaching and learning in the light of observed pupil learning in research lessons that are often repeated (Dudley, 2010).

In the interviewing of pupils

If the intended beneficiaries of a lesson are the children then there is obvious benefit in hearing their opinions on what they learned and what helped them learn (and what got in their way). The power of the interviews comes from the directness of the feedback, both in time (immediately after the lesson – much will be lost for adults if the interviews are left any later, but with a delay the children may well forget, confuse or substitute their experiences if they have had intervening lessons) and in style ('the first part was really interesting and helped me with my multiplication but the second part was just boring').

Some schools are concerned that the presence of the teacher who taught the lesson may affect the feedback given as children worry about being polite about the lesson, for example. One way round this is to record (with the children's consent) the feedback in answer to questions posed by other members of the Lesson Study group. This enables the child's exact words to be heard by the teacher who gave the lesson (and reduces the temptation for 'translation' by one teacher to another later – 'he said that the first part was really interesting and helped him with his multiplication but that the second part . . . began to lose pace'). It also enables the Lesson Study group to rewind or pause in discussion of the children's responses, which isn't possible when the children are in the room.

Of course, the benefits of such interviews with children are not only for the teachers, but for the pupils themselves. Being asked to reflect on their learning, what helped and what could help even more next time, develops the learning-to-learn skills that will support the children's development far beyond the lesson in question. The first time you ask children such questions they may have difficulty in answering, but in schools where Lesson Study is well established children have been given 'speaking frames' to structure their feedback, the questions are used routinely as part of the plenary session in class, and this language is a familiar classroom idiom.

In the post-lesson discussion . . .

Fundamental to the success of Lesson Study are the skills of reflection and questioning of one's own and each other's practice, and the beliefs and assumptions on which this practice is built. Such intrapersonal skills are related to but separate from the skills in teaching, so that it is possible to be adept in these areas while less experienced or less effective as a teacher. The impact of a Lesson Study will be dependent not only on the pedagogical abilities of those taking part in the study, but on their skills in interrogating their pedagogy. Equally, the process of Lesson Study will develop these intrapersonal skills and habits of reflective practice in the teachers taking part, and thus contribute to this aspect of their professional development, as well as their understanding of the particular pedagogical issue under scrutiny. At the end of a Lesson Study the participants will be better teachers but also better at asking questions about teaching.

In the passing on of the knowledge arrived at . . .

The act of passing on to others the new knowledge that these teachers have developed seems to 'fix' it in their conscious as well as unconscious minds and to make it more accessible for future use.

The positive impact of Lesson Study seems to be because it combines a unique mix of processes that are all conducive to teacher learning. The learning is contextualised and there is (Dudley, 2009):

• a collaborative focus on specific learners;

- multiple perspectives of learners' learning;
- collaborative, recursive construction and analysis of learning for specific pupils in their classrooms in research lessons; and
- the passing on to other professionals of the new practice knowledge discovered.

LS has been demonstrated to improve learning outcomes for pupils in large-scale studies of schools using LS as a process of continuing professional learning (Hadfield et al, 2011; Dudley, 2012 forthcoming).

Lesson Study and initial teacher training

Increasingly, LS processes are being used as a means to improve professional learning in the initial training of teachers and of recently qualified teachers. In Japan LS plays a key role in the induction year of teachers. We have looked at how LS is developing in a small number of higher education teacher training courses in England and Northern Ireland as well as in the United States of America where it is in more widespread use.

Based upon his detailed study of how teachers learn in LS contexts, Dudley (2011d) suggests that the principles from LS learning be applied to designs for your trainee learning during school placements. In addition to providing opportunities for you to practise your teaching, any placement should also build in opportunities for trainees to participate in lesson studies with the teachers in the placement schools. These lesson studies would, ideally, be conducted with children of different ages, and address different curricular or subject areas. On longer degree courses, the lesson studies might, over time, focus in on areas of teaching in which you have experienced the most difficulties or have amassed least experience. Participating in LS learning with experienced teachers would provide opportunities for you to learn in LS zones of proximal teacher development that Dudley's study has identified. It would allow you access to the tacit knowledge of more experienced colleagues and enable them to go through the detailed, imagined, and observed micro-level practices that LS involves.

We are arguing here for opportunities to be created for trainees to conduct Lesson Studies with teachers in placement schools. Some researchers report successes in using LS among groups of ITT students alone (Hiebert, 2005; Fernandez, 2004). However, while many of the attributes of LS make this a valuable approach, the danger of pooled inexperience cannot be ignored. Some studies have suggested that groups of pre-service teachers can derive benefit from aspects of LS such as comparing the predicted and observed learning (Fernandez, 2009; Parks, 2008), but others document such intense intervention and instruction from course tutors that the integrity of the LS process seems significantly compromised (Puchner and Taylor, 2006; Sims, and Walsh, 2009).

Trainees and those who support them might consider the multiple models possible for structuring Lesson Study, including those that are possible only because of the unique opportunities deriving from initial teacher training contexts. For example:

1. Two or more trainees carry out a Lesson Study during their school-based placement.

2. One or more trainees in one school carry out a Lesson Study with one or more trainees in another school.

3. One or more trainees carry out a Lesson Study together with one or more of their school-based mentors.

4. One or more trainees work on a Lesson Study together with one or more of their school-based mentors and university-based tutor.

Activity:

What do you see as the advantages and disadvantages of each the four models suggested above? Which model do you think would be most practicable for you?

Model 1 (two or more trainees carry out a Lesson Study during their school-based placement). This has the *advantages* of practicality. It is a model that has been used by many teacher training institutions to make a virtue of the necessity of paired placements in contexts where there is a difficulty in finding a separate class for each to be on placement.

The *disadvantage* of this model is the extent to which it is dependent on your skills not just in teaching but in interrogating your teaching. As we have said, these skills are separate from the skills of pedagogy, and as an inexperienced trainee you may still bring to bear on a pedagogical discussion resources such as:

• the intrapersonal skills and habits of reflecting on performance;

• careful and objective observation skills enabling clarity about what is really happening in a classroom;

• skilful ways to question yourself and others about the reasons why things happen the way they do in the human interaction that are the context for learning.

However, these are habits and ways of working that are closely linked to teaching and there is the chance that a more experienced teacher will have a greater degree of skill in these areas. By restricting participation in the Lesson Study to only trainees, as in this model, there is the potential (though by no means the certainty) of losing the pedagogical knowledge and good approaches for arriving at that knowledge which experienced teachers could bring.

Model 2 (one or more trainees in one school carry out a Lesson Study with one or more trainees in another school). This has the same potential *disadvantages* as the first model, and it doesn't have the advantages of practicality. If you and your peers are in separate schools you have the logistical challenges of distance and timetabling for making time and space for the

Lesson Study. However, it has other *advantages*. By opening up the doors not only of another classroom but the doors of another school, participants in the Lesson Study double the number of schools they have professional contact with. By seeing a different way of doing things and glimpsing a different culture, they are better able to isolate the features that create the culture in their own placement school. We saw in the EPPI systematic review of the features of successful collaborative professional learning that external input is a critical feature for positive impact on teaching and learning, and this model incorporates such external expertise. If you are the only one on placement in a school, constructing a Lesson Study in this way can also reduce any sense of isolation you might feel.

Model 3 (one or more trainees carry out a Lesson Study together with one or more of their school-based mentors). This has the *advantages* of building shared understandings about teaching between the two participants in the crucial mentor–trainee relationship. And since the skills for effective Lesson Study are very similar to the skills needed for effective mentoring, the process is likely to support mentors to be better in their role even once the Lesson Study is over.

A *disadvantage* of this model is in the difficulty for both you and your mentor setting aside the assessment role that mentors are required to have over the course of your placement. Lesson Study is most powerful when participants are looking into an area of practice where they are dissatisfied with what they are achieving. It may be hard for a mentor to relinquish their position as 'expert' and engage in collaborative enquiry in an area where teaching is not as successful as they would like it to be. Even more so, it requires a very brave trainee to open up these areas of their practice to scrutiny by the person who will ultimately be responsible for passing judgement on the overall quality of their teaching. Even if both you and your mentor agree and are able to set aside these judgements and roles, it may be hard to let go of the idioms and vocabulary and habits that go with an assessment function (particularly the tendency to focus on teaching rather than learning; the 'performance' at the front of the class, rather than the shifts in understanding among the 'audience'). Lesson Study is a much more profound activity than simply agreeing whether a particular lesson was 'good' or not.

Of course, if these obstacles can be surmounted, the resulting relationship between you and your mentor is likely to be based on more deeply held and understood views on the learning process, and the benefits will be enormous, not only to both parties' teaching, but also to your mentoring relationship.

One way that some schools have managed this challenge to bring additional benefits is by organising the processes of Lesson Study with two trainee–mentor pairs. If trainee A is usually supported by mentor A and trainee B by mentor B, in the Lesson Study it is mentor B who works with trainee A and likewise mentor A who works with trainee B. The skills of mentoring, and learning conversations are still being developed through the Lesson Study and the process results not only in trainees and mentors who are better teachers but in mentors who are better mentors.

Model 4 (one or more trainees work on a Lesson Study together with one or more of their school-based mentors and university-based tutor). This is a powerful approach to Lesson Study, drawing on the different perspectives and resources of different agents in the process of initial teacher training. It also has the *advantage* of giving a concrete and shared context for discussions about pedagogy for people who may be from different backgrounds and traditions, and it is the best way of bringing to the Lesson Study the external expertise identified in the research (Cordingley et al, 2003) as a crucial ingredient for effective collaborative learning. Of course, the logistics necessary to co-ordinate the availability of an external university-based tutor may be such a large *disadvantage* as to make this model a rarity.

Use of video

One technique that has been used to manage some of the logistical challenges which can be present in any approach to Lesson Study, and that is particularly appropriate for initial teacher training, is the use of video. Adrian Copping discusses the use of video more generally in your training in Chapter 3; however, its appropriateness for Lesson Study in initial teacher training contexts lies in the fact that even with optimum technical conditions (not always available on limited IT budgets and in the echoing rooms of old school buildings), video is not an ideal way to capture what is going on in a lesson. In a class of 30, a video records only a small percentage of the interactions and epiphanies that take place at any one time. However, in a small group context a mounted video can capture a much higher percentage of what is going on, and is an adequate substitute for a human eye. Of course, it has the advantage over the human eye that what it records can be shared, stopped, rewound, paused and discussed as an external artefact after the event. If trainees are working with a small group out of class then video can be used to record the teaching and learning; then later it can be watched and discussed together with other members of the Lesson Study group. This removes the need to timetable all other members of the Lesson Study group to be free from teaching responsibilities at the same time, and there is little impact on the quality of what is recorded in the observations of the lesson; there is the same careful scrutiny of practice but it is asynchronous with the lesson taking place. Of course, the video also enables you as the teacher to observe your own lesson, which brings significant benefits to the quality of discussion.

Conclusions

Given all of this, we would argue that LS should form the basis of continuing teacher learning for newly qualified teachers in their induction training in school. Dudley's study suggests that use of LS as a model for Newly Qualified Teacher (NQT) learning in the induction year could not only improve the teaching of the NQT but also improve the quality of the work of induction tutors. It is likely that engagement in such Lesson Studies would provide trainees with material and experiences that can be written up reflectively as part of their course requirements. In this way LS can be seen to offer new teachers a grounding in reflective practice that could help more teachers to remain reflective in the course of their post-induction teaching, and this could be harnessed as a basis for formal classroom research, contributing to formal accredited learning, such as a master's level qualification.

In summary, then, all of these elements of ITT and induction offer possibilities for centre-based training organisations as well as SCITTS and EBTTS to interact with placement schools in order to help teachers to create more effective learning during teaching placement. These could strengthen the links between university education departments and schools. LS could also, in this way, offer potential models for design for the professional learning of trainees in another current policy development: university training schools (DfE 2010). One final outcome might even be that future teachers, accustomed to using LS as their default mode of professional learning, might also see practitioner research as a natural next step and engage more readily in master's programmes.

Learning Outcomes Review

This chapter sets Lesson Study in the context of the theories and research into how we use talk in learning, reflective practice, effective professional learning and encouraging and listening to pupil voices for teacher learning, as well as setting out the historical context for this approach to professional learning and the way that it has developed in Japan.

The following seven elements make up one 'Lesson Study cycle':
1. Identifying a focus.
2. Identifying case pupils.
3. Planning a research lesson.
4. Conducting the research lesson and gathering evidence of the pupils' learning – particularly the case pupils.
5. Interviewing case pupils (and sometimes other pupils) about the research lesson.
6. Conducting a post-lesson discussion to review the pupils' learning and to begin to identify points for the next research lesson.
7. Passing on to others what has been learned by the Lesson Study group and capturing this on record.

Teachers can learn most by repeating this cycle three or more times addressing the same issue.

Initial teacher training contexts offer rich opportunities for using Lesson Study and the chapter also suggests some models and the potential advantages and drawbacks of each.

Self assessment questions
1. Identify some of the connections and differences between Lesson Study and other forms of professional learning you have experienced. Can you identify features of Lesson Study that will encourage you to try this approach to professional learning?

2. Review the seven elements of Lesson Study. Identify which of them are processes that would be new to you and/or the people you work with.
3. How might you use Lesson Study in your current professional learning context within the next few months?

Further Reading

Yoshida, M. (2002) *Lesson Study: An Introduction*. Global Education Resources, NJ.
The work of Makoto Yoshida was one of the first people to bring the concept of LS to the West. His introduction to LS is a must-read.

Lewis, C. (1998) A lesson is like a swiftly flowing river: how research lessons improve Japanese education. *American Educator*, Winter: 12–17, 50–1.

Lewis, C., Perry, R. and Hurd, J. (2004) A deeper look at lesson study. *Educational Leadership*, 61(5): 18–22.

Lewis, C., Perry, R. and Murata, A. (2006) How should research contribute to instructional improvement? The case of lesson study. *Education Researcher,* 35(3): 3–14.

Likewise, the work of Catherine Lewis is highly accessible and informative. Catherine was one of the first western educators to write about LS, having researched it in Japan and developed it in the USA at Mills College, working a lot with pre-service teachers as well as serving teachers.

For developments in LS in the UK the best resource is Dudley's online Lesson Study handbook (2011c), which brings together and updates work over ten years developing LS in a national pilot (NCSL 2005) and subsequently with the National Strategies (DCSF 2008) and through his Teaching and Learning Research Programme (TLRP) work (summarised on the TLRP website: www.tlrp.ac.uk and in Dudley 2011a). All these resources and more are brought together at www.lessonstudy.co.uk

References

Cordingley, P., Bell, M., Rundell, B. and Evans, D. (2003) The impact of collaborative CPD on classroom teaching and learning. In *Research Evidence in Education Library*. London: EPPI-Centre, Social Science Research Unit, Institute of Education, University of London.

Department for Children, Schools and Families (2008) *Improving Practice and Progression Through Lesson Study: A Handbook for Headteachers, Leading Teachers and Subject Leaders.* London: DCSF.

Dudley, P. (2007) *The Lesson Study Professional Learning Approach*. Teaching and Learning Update. London: Optimus.

Dudley, P. (2010) How teachers learn in lesson study contexts. Paper presented at the annual conference of the British Educational Research Association, Warwick University, 4 September.

Dudley, P. (2011a) *Lesson Study: What it is, How and Why it Works and Who is Using it*. Teaching and Learning Update. London: Optimus.

Dudley, P. (2011b) *Lesson Study Toolkit*. Bethlehem: Bethlehem University.

Dudley, P. (2011c) *Lesson Study: A Handbook*. Available at: www.lessonstudy.co.uk (accessed 25/3/12).

Dudley, P. (2011d) Unpublished PhD thesis, Cambridge.

Dudley, P. (2012, forthcoming) How Lesson Study contributed to a national strategy for improving teaching. *International Journal of Lesson Studies*, 1(1).

Fernandez, M. L. (2004) Learning though modified lesson study in a teacher preparation course. Paper presented at the Annual Conference of the American Educational Research Association, San Diego, California.

GTCE (2003) Vygotsky's ideas on teaching and learning. Available through: www.canterbury.ac.uk/ (accessed 3/4/12).

Hadfield, M., Jopling, M. and Emira, M. (2011) *Evaluation of the National Strategies Primary Leading Teachers Programme*. University of Wolverhampton.

Hiebert, J. (2005) *Alternative Teacher Preparation: Learning to Learn to Teach Mathematics*. University of Delaware.

Lewis, C. (1998) A lesson is like a swiftly flowing river: how research lessons improve Japanese education. *American Educator*, Winter: 12–17, 50–1.

Lewis, C., Perry, R. and Hurd, J. (2004) A deeper look at lesson study. *Educational Leadership*, 61(5): 18–22.

Lewis, C., Perry, R. and Murata, A. (2006) How should research contribute to instructional improvement? The case of lesson study. *Education Researcher*, 35(3): 3–14.

Macintyre, D., Pedder, D. and Rudduck, J, (2007) Pupil voice: comfortable and uncomfortable learnings for teachers. *Research Papers in Education*. 20(2).

McKinsey and Co. (2007) *How the World's Top Performing School Systems Come Out on Top*. London: McKinsey & Co.

McKinsey and Co. (2010) *How the World's Most Improved School Systems Keep Getting Better*. London: McKinsey & Co.

NCSL (2005) *Getting Started with Networked Research Lesson Study*. Nottingham: National College for School Leadership.

Parks, A. (2008) Messy learning: preservice teachers' lesson study conversations. *Teaching and Teacher Education*, 24(5): 1200–16.

Puchner, L. and Taylor, D. (2006) Lesson study and teacher efficacy: stories from two school based lesson study groups. *Teaching and Teacher Education*, 22(7): 922–34.

Rudduck, J. and Flutter, J. (2010) Pupil participation and pupil perspective: carving a new order of experience. *Cambridge Journal of Education*, 30(1).

Schön, D. (1983) *The Reflective Practitioner: How Professionals Think in Action*. New York: Basic Books.

Sims, L. and Walsh, D. (2009) Lesson study with pre-service teachers: lessons from lessons. *Teaching and Teacher Education*, 25: 724–33.

Vygotsky, L. (1986) *Thought and Language*. MIT Press.

Yoshida, M. (2002) *Lesson Study: An Introduction*. Global Education Resources, NJ.

8. Reflective journals and portfolios
Helen Davenport

Learning Outcomes

By the end of this chapter you will:

- have developed a deeper understanding of the benefits of reflecting through the act of writing;
- have gained strategies for starting to write and developing the criticality within your writing;
- have greater insight into the barriers to reflective writing and how they might be overcome;
- be aware of other 'sites' of reflection, beyond a written journal.

Becoming an effective writer

In the course of learning to teach, reflection is not a word that you are likely to avoid. I have (thankfully) yet to meet a teacher who would say that they are not reflective, or that they don't reflect on their teaching regularly. And yet, they don't all keep learning journals. Schön (1987) identifies that practitioners reflect on what they do as they go about their practice, thinking on their feet, calling this *reflection-in-action*. But, just as important, are the thoughtful reflections we engage in once we are away from the immediacy of key moments in practice. It is here that we might ponder on events as we drive home, or talk things through with a colleague or partner. This *reflection-on-action*, it could be argued, is 'in-the-head reflection', which Moore and Ash (2002) suggest can be a very deep kind of reflecting. However, their study suggests that while 'in-the-head' reflection is effective, it can be made far more powerful when supported by writing (2002, p.8).

In my role as a teacher educator, I have become increasingly passionate about the power of the written word and its ability to harness our thoughts and view them through a multitude of different lenses. The aim of this chapter is to convey the potency and magic of reflective writing, encouraging you to take stock of where, how and when you stand back and attempt to make sense of your practice. It is worth noting at this stage that this section has been born out of working very closely with my own trainees. Through listening to their experiences of writing reflectively, I have gained a deeper realisation of the barriers that so often present themselves on the journey to becoming a reflective writer. Committing to reflect deeply on your practice through reflective writing will require some thought, planning and time. It will ask you to challenge your own thinking and question the seemingly ordinary. As my own trainees have immersed themselves into reflecting on their practice through writing they have often surprised themselves:

> So I just started writing and then I found I couldn't stop writing. I wrote three whole pages and it goes on and on in my journal, asking questions and wandering off on tangents. As I wrote, I started to think of new ways of thinking about the incident in the playground . . . it helped me to think of ways forward for the next day

(Kelly, BA Year 2 Trainee)

> Sometimes when you're writing, you realise you've never thought of it that way and then you suddenly think – actually that is a really good idea and that thought might change a lot for you and make your practice better, make you kind of understand it in a way you never have before.

(Sarah, PGCE Trainee)

Hopefully, these snippets of conversations with trainees, offer a glimpse of the 'magic' of reflective writing that I've alluded to. What now follows is an attempt to give a rich insight into how engaging with reflective writing and activities can be highly beneficial throughout your journey in becoming a reflective teacher. We will initially consider how you might begin to engage with reflective writing, addressing practical aspects of getting started and finding the time. The notion of the writing as an important event in its own right will be explored, together with a close look at how to develop pieces of reflective writing further, making the most of their potential. The lived realities of being a reflective writer will also be unpicked, with a consideration of the pitfalls that can arise and how you might work your way through them. If you feel particularly resistant to the idea of journal writing, then there are a number of alternative 'places' suggested, that you might identify with more readily.

Why write it down?

In the introductory section, we arrived at a juncture whereby teachers naturally reflect and ponder on their practice and pedagogies, and that this 'in-the-head' reflection could be harnessed and enriched by committing such thoughts to paper. Such reflecting *on* actions lends itself beautifully to journal writing, with writing being said to provide 'a means of puzzling through what is happening in our work and personal lives' (Boud, 2001, p.11). As such, it is easy to see how learning journals have become the tool to facilitate the development of reflective practice and thus are so commonly used in teacher education courses. It is this fascinating process of 'puzzling through' that I urge you to use your writing space for, rather than writing merely because it is a requirement of your course.

The thoughts we have about our ongoing practice, the dilemmas, the moments of surprise, anger, intrigue or joy, are often fleeting and caught up in emotions. In our heads, they drift along, perhaps being made some sense of or re-edited to lessen their weight. In the busy day-to-day lives of being a teacher, they may simply evaporate and travel little distance. But if these thoughts can be captured through writing and placed on the page it becomes possible to observe them more closely. The journal entry could be considered a valuable artefact and one that can be plundered for meaning in a far deeper way than we can ever do with thought alone.

But what is this mysterious 'meaning' that you should be attempting to find in your writing? Bolton (2010, p.7) states that in their most compelling forms, reflective writings have the capacity to be 'transgressive of stable and controlling orders; they lead cogs to decide to change shape, change place, even configure whole new systems'.

When considering my own experiences with reflective writing, I identify with this notion, recognising the potential potency that such reflective practice has to disrupt and challenge thinking. It allows us to tip things on their head, look at them from different perspectives and through different lenses, developing our critical thoughts and responses. From one encounter or scenario you have experienced and written about, a new consideration or approach may emerge, thus turning reflective thought into reflexive action. And so, with this heady potential in mind, let us turn to the task in hand and focus on getting started.

Getting started

So far, I have referred to those intangible moments that the reflective writing paradigm dangles towards us – the 'carrot' of critical thought, of shifts in thinking and reimagined future practice. The playful use of 'magic' has alluded to the almost mythical qualities that such moments have, so hard are they to pin down. What I have discovered by listening to tales of writing, though, is that there is often another elusive element present – the sheer motivation to put thoughts into text.

Motivation

> The thing that always stopped me from writing was ... well, I can just sit there and just not know what to write at all. Or because sometimes I get home from Uni and I just can't be bothered. I get home and I just want to sleep. I can think about those things on the bus and be sure I want to write about that, but then, it just doesn't happen.

> (Katie, BA Primary Year 3 trainee)

Here, Katie has tapped into, quite honestly, the commonplace case of 'I just can't quite be bothered'. The good intentions were there on the bus, but never quite materialised! These are motivational issues that I readily identify with; sitting down to compose a journal entry is something that can easily become shunted out of the day, even if there is every intention to write. Clearly, in order to reap some of the benefits of journal writing, writing needs to take place in the first instance. For some people this will come easily and may even be second nature, particularly if journal or diary writing has been a pleasurable and rewarding activity in the past. For others, though, this may not feel as enticing. So – how can we circumnavigate this initial barrier of journal apathy?

Identifying time to write

My own approach to ensuring that I commit to regular writing has been to carefully plan and allocate time for it to happen. It is also useful to have an idea of how many journal entries you would like to write in a given time-frame, if you suspect this writing time might vanish. So, for example, I aim to write at least one substantial journal entry a week, usually yielding 12 entries over a term. More frequent, shorter entries may feel more suitable for you. For some, though, this may feel too procedural and you might prefer to take a more spontaneous approach, writing with immediacy, in response to something that has really fired your thinking. You could even adopt both of these approaches. The intention of this advice is simply to highlight that in order to make sense of your reflective writing, it is a process that needs to actually happen! You may find that setting times and goals can support you in this.

The journal

Let us consider now the form that this journal might take. For me, the luxury of new, attractive stationery, has an enduring appeal. I find the act of writing with a fountain pen on a clean page highly alluring – but this isn't for everyone. I have seen journals take many different forms. Many of my trainees use word processing or phone applications to compile their entries. Others use A4 loose-leaf files, whereby entries can be added or removed, depending on the context in which they are being shared. Some trainees prefer larger, scrapbook-style portfolios. These allow them to present their writings together with photographs from school, sketches or mind-maps. Whatever medium you choose, it should call to you and invite you to use it.

Research Focus

Lee (2010) explored the effectiveness of an interactive online journalling tool in enhancing the quality of reflection in Physical Education teacher trainees. Each trainee was asked to select a journal partner and form a reflection 'dyad', writing journal entries and commenting on each other's writing. Participants in this study reported that this online shared journal approach had been very helpful in providing a critical friend who could ask challenging questions and offer suggestions and ideas. The social support that this provided was also noted as useful. This research helps to support the anecdotal comments from my own trainees that the use of both online communication and peer support can enrich and further the reflective writing process. There are several web tools that are useful in facilitating this approach (or for your own individual journalling). Penzu and PebblePad are both visually attractive and engaging and allow your journal entries to be shared with others.

It is important to recognise that just as we acknowledge the different learning styles and preferences of our learners, we need to acknowledge that we will have preferred styles of reflecting. For some of my trainees, none of the above media have felt notably inspiring. I have considered it my role, as their tutor, to find a way in that *does* appeal. Alternative sites of reflection, such as blogs, podcasts and digitally recorded discussion groups, have proved more motivating to some trainees and allowed them to find a space that feels relevant and useful for their reflections. Another popular space has been the use of forums or ongoing e-mail conversations using social networking and messenger sites.

Case Study

Katie had found committing to journal writing very difficult and found it hard to become motivated to write. In one tutor-led session, a discussion on inclusive practice gained interest and considerable momentum in Katie's group. There were a lot of interesting points made, from a range of different perspectives, and a rather lively debate ensued. As we had been interrogating spaces for reflection earlier in the session, one member of the group volunteered to open a conversation thread on an online social network, to allow the discussion to continue. Over the following week, this online conversation flowed easily, with all members of the group contributing. The original discussion rapidly evolved and the thread began to cover a variety of issues and concerns that the trainees had, relating to aspects of inclusion in the classroom.

For Katie, this discussion thread became her space for writing in a reflective way, with the helpful addition of being able to bounce her ideas and thinking off her peers. She printed her contributions to the conversation and kept them in a portfolio. As the term went on, Katie started to explore these writings and developed her ideas in more extended, individual entries. For her, this collaborative discussion in an online community had provided a 'way in'. Beyond being a space that gave Katie the impetus to write, it also provided somewhere that felt 'safe' to express her ideas and wonderings. As she recalls:

I actually found it much easier to say what I was thinking than I do in sessions. It gave me the time to think about my reply carefully and to reflect on what others were saying and how this related to my own ideas – some of the conversations really made me stop and think. I suddenly realised that I was writing so much and that I had a lot to say! It gave me the confidence and motivation to go on to write my own reflective pieces but I still continue to get a lot from the forum discussions.

Igniting the writing

Once you have carved out the time in which you intend to write, you will inevitably find yourself gazing towards a blank piece of paper or screen. Rather than be deterred by the vacuum before you, regard this as a space where interesting things can happen! I've spent a lot of time listening to my trainees about what makes them want to write and what they write about. In most instances, the crucial factor is an 'ignition' – something potent that is deemed worthy of writing about.

> *I found that comment from the teacher really touched a nerve, it made me think about my own experiences in school and my confidence in maths. There were sparks started for me there, a real personal interest that I* needed *to write about.*

> (Jo, PGCE trainee)

It is difficult here to be too prescriptive about what will provide writing ignition for you, but I urge you to watch out for these flickers of intrigue and wonder and endeavour to follow up any 'sparks' that get lit, through your writing. What ignites the urge to write is a rather individual and elusive ingredient. For Jo, her own experiences and an off-the-cuff comment from a teacher really got her thinking. It may be that you read something that triggers a flurry of thinking, or you may choose to use your writing space as a cathartic outlet for an event that has proved rather difficult or emotive. As a first point of call, try to gravitate towards moments that have recently grabbed your attention or made you intrigued. It may be that you choose to reflect on something that has happened in the staffroom, classroom or playground. You might want to revisit a conversation you have had in a university session or some reading on an educational issue. If you have a particular spark, run with it, aiming to write in a relatively free style form to begin with. Set yourself an allocated amount of time, or number of words. You will probably find that you end up writing far more than you anticipated! This 'stream of consciousness' writing tends to evolve and go on a journey of its own.

It may be that these moments don't always present themselves so readily, in which case you may find it helpful to give yourself something a little more prescriptive, if free-flow writing feels rather daunting. However, if you have set aside the time to write and nothing in particular has really fired your thinking, it is useful to have some other ways in and I provide a few examples in the activity below.

Activity
Ideas for Ignition
You could try one of the following to get you going.
- Rewrite an encounter in the classroom from the pupil's perspective.
- Write a letter to someone who has got you thinking this week (a parent, a peer, a teacher from your past?).
- On your journey to becoming a teacher, what has inspired you/surprised you/shocked you/upset you?
- If you could have three wishes in education, what would they be?
- Describe the kind of teacher you are, to a future class.

- What has been the highlight (or lowlight, if your mood so inclines) of your teaching career to date?
- Imagine your teaching in the classroom you were in today; as an observer looking from above – what did you see?
- Reflect on what you have been learning about in your teaching sessions this week. What one thing really stood out and why?

My advice would be to just go for it, without stopping to think too much about what you want to write. The beauty of journal writing is that it needn't be rehearsed; indeed for me, the most useful reflections often surge from what I had perceived to be a drought!

The writing event

It is easy to see the written journal entry as the item of significance. In many ITT settings, there will be a clear requirement for you to write and keep a reflective learning journal or portfolio, with these being assessed in some instances. I would, however, like to highlight the significance of the writing process, or 'event'. I contend that the very process of writing can be transformative – in that we think as we write. As we write, we are prompted to explore other avenues, and, hopefully, we are able to respond to our own questions. A journal can be seen as an ongoing conversation, where the author is both 'the learner and the one who teaches' (Holly 1989, p.14). Bolton argues that deep insight can be gained by this dynamic, self-dialogic process, insight that could not be gained by verbal discussion with peers or mentors alone – whereby 'the writer is face to face with themselves' (2010, p.129). Therefore, I would encourage you to consider the *process* of writing as important, rather than as a means to an end product.

> *I found that writing things down was different from just telling someone about it. I was able to really lay down my thoughts – it exposed them and made them more transparent. As I write, I usually have some kind of realisation, if you like; I start to gain a new understanding of what might actually be happening. It often starts off as something quite emotional but by the end of the writing session, it begins to make a calmer sort of sense.*

> (Neelam, BA Year 4 trainee)

Neelam's arrival at a 'calmer sort of sense' can be seen, if not as overt reflexive action, then at least as powerful reflective activity. What I'm aiming to highlight here is that it isn't just the end product that is of importance, and this is an aspect of reflective writing that can be easily overlooked.

A reoccurring phenomenon in my trainee's tales of reflective writing is that of the 'unleashed' words, whereby the author begins to write and finds it difficult to stop. So, as you get ready to launch into the act of making time to sit and write, remember that this process brings its own rewards – it isn't just a means to an end product. What transformative qualities await will be unique and personal to you and will undoubtedly differ each time you engage with the process. It is worthwhile to step back and ponder on what you have gained from each piece. Have you moved nearer to a resolution? Do you feel calmer? Or have you raised some pertinent questions that you would like to address?

How to develop the writing further

Research Focus

Dyment and O'Connell (2010) attempt to shed light on the conflicts existing in the literature surrounding the quality of reflection in trainee reflective journals. They note that some research found trainee journals to contain deeply reflective writing. However, other research painted a more pessimistic picture, revealing that the majority of writing was mostly of the descriptive nature, with little evidence of critical reflection. Their study reviews a wide range of literature on reflective writing and uses this to identify what they consider to limit or enable student writing to be highly reflective. The review explores a range of aspects such as the impact of clarity of expectations and assessment, modelling and relationships with lecturers. As such, it provides a useful insight into where trainees struggle with their writing, highlighting a number of helpful ways in which these struggles may be supported or overcome.

Getting started with the writing is a big step, but once reflective writing becomes an established activity for you (or even after your first few attempts) it is useful to stand back and consider where your writing is taking you and how you can develop it further. The qualities that your reflective writings include are important. The writing process should continue to move you forward with your thinking and practice, rather than taking you round in circles of unresolved logic or dumping you at a dead end.

The first main checkpoint here would be to consider your writing in terms of what it is achieving. It needs to go beyond just *describing* what you did, what you saw, thought or read, moving towards a more critical means of reflecting. This isn't always easy. If the blank page does get the better of you, your writing can end up as a simple retelling of an event or moment of learning. While this may have some use as a record, it probably isn't going to take your thinking on much further.

Case Study

Mark, a BA Year 2 trainee, engaged with journal writing on a fairly regular basis, using the space to write about his sessions.

October 5th

In today's session, we learned about the different ways that we can respond to diversity. One of these was to ignore differences, another was to treat difference as a problem and another was to celebrate difference and treat diversity as an asset. We also learned about how diversity can come in many different forms and that there are hidden and surface differences in any classroom. In the follow-up seminar we discussed how these issues were relevant to our school experience.

Mark brought his journal writing to me, unsure as to where it was taking him. While recording notes like this may be a useful record of learning, it wasn't allowing Mark to really grapple with any of these issues or to add his own thoughts or ideas. As such, the writing felt empty and lacking in any reflective activity or 'wonderings'. I encouraged him to revisit what we had discussed in the session. Had this reminded him of any examples from his own practice during school-based training or of observations he had made? Did any particular children come to mind or had any peer discussions about this issue got him thinking? Mark admitted that journal writing about his own thoughts and feelings made him feel quite at sea, but agreed to give it a go.

October 12th

Piotr, though originally from Poland, seemed to fit in well with class but was as capable as any other child. My instinct had been to leave him to it and not make a fuss. My discussions in the session last week have made me wonder a bit more about this experience. Using the framework introduced in the lecture, I was trying to avoid seeing Piotr as a problem. However, now I wonder whether simply ignoring hidden differences can be seen as problematic as making an issue out of them. By ignoring Piotr's 'Polishness' was I also denying a part of him that was important to his identity?

What are your impressions of these two pieces of writing? How would you encourage Mark to take his ideas even further?

Mark's second journal entry feels far more 'useful' in terms of where this might take him forward with his thinking and practice. There are a number of avenues that open up here, relating to how Mark might begin to reframe his approach, together with pursuing theoretical ideas that have helped to shape his ideas.

Committing thoughts to paper, particularly if these are to be shared with peers and tutors (something that will be addressed shortly), can be unnerving. It may feel 'safer' to write a closed and descriptive piece. There are a number of frameworks and typologies that can offer you support in developing increasing levels of criticality in your reflective journal writing (see Further Reading). However, it is worth noting that while frameworks of writing attempt to demonstrate what differing levels of sophistication in criticality might look like, reflective writing doesn't always fit into neat categories – particularly when there is an undercurrent of emotion or a fervent need to ask questions. However, the writing *should* be taking you on a forward trajectory – it should be making you think things through analytically, using different lenses or pushing you to explore *why* you feel a certain way about events or issues.

Hopefully you are gaining a sense that reflective writing should feel worthwhile. In the early stages, try not to worry too much about the sophistication of your writing. Indeed, I encourage my trainees to write whatever they can to begin with. If this does end up being a recount of a session or event then no matter, at least the act of writing has been established and we have something to work with!

Activity
Taking stock of your writing – a review of your journal entries so far
Take a look at some of your writing so far, particularly if you haven't revisited any entries yet. The following prompts might help you to probe further and consider where you could take your writing next.
- Have you been able to write about your own personal experiences in the classroom or are you discussing the practice of others?
- Whose voice has more weight in your writing? Is it your own or can you hear the voice of your tutor? Your class teacher? Your mentor? Your parents? Your peers? If so, how could you make *your* voice have more resonance?
- Take a highlighter and identify where you have asked any unanswered questions. Have you been able to move towards a resolution, or a way forward with them? Would additional reading or discussions with peers/tutors/colleagues support you with this?
- Can you spot any themes arising throughout your entries?
- Are there any aspects of your writing that you no longer feel the same about?
- Is there anything you would like to say, but haven't had the confidence to?
- Which piece of writing took you on the furthest journey?
- Can you identify places in your writing where you had a 'light bulb' moment? What happened as a result?

If any of these prompts strike a chord, make the most of this spark and use the ignition to pursue further writings.

The aftermath – how to make the most of your writing

You have sat down and written a journal entry, thrashing through the issues and events that have been of significance that week. Now what? The activity above asked you to revisit your writing and take stock. I consider this to be a particularly important aspect of the reflective writing process. Sometimes, when reflective writing is used to offload pent-up feeling or emotions, there can be a reluctance to expose ourselves to the text at a later date. However, if the writing is put to bed and left alone, is it being fully utilised and explored?

The private event of journalling offers space to work through and reflect upon encounters that are often messy and confused. It allows the author to 'step back' and look closely at these happenings and perhaps start to make sense of vulnerable thoughts and emotions. From this may come a consideration of how things may be approached differently – or a heightened awareness of the broader discourses that such a moment may be situated within. In this sense, we can regard the reflective journal as a venue for discharging emotions so that we may move forward. While I maintain that this unfolding process is highly significant in its own right, I suggest that there may also be danger lurking in the solitary writing experience. Without the voice of the 'other' – peers, tutors, a mentor – is it always possible to reflect meaningfully on the resulting writing? And is the writing sometimes in jeopardy of being used as a dumping ground for emotions, without pause for critical refrain?

Undoubtedly, the private space of the journal lends itself to the unloading of powerful emotions, particularly those that emerge in the demands of school based training.

> *Last year on placement I taught a girl who behaved in a very challenging way, but only in the lessons I took. It was hard not take it personally. I ended up writing a whole page of a complete rant about our failing relationship. I sat there for more than an hour, writing about what a horrible day I'd had and how I felt. Then I put it to one side and that was it, release. I didn't look back on it again.*

> *(Trish, PGCE student)*

I refer to this kind of writing as the 'angry page', whereby the writing space is used to deposit frustrations of the moment. While the act of 'releasing' negative emotions may have been helpful to some extent, was Trish able to maximise this process through self-dialogue, 'face to face' with herself, as Bolton (2010) suggests? There is the possibility here that the writing may well have been a very heated and passionate recount of events, rather than a careful consideration of where this relationship was going wrong and how it might be moved forward. I would argue that the abrupt (or passive) casting aside of writing – while understandable – may well limit the capacity to reflect deeply on what is at play with feelings, ideas and situations. If the writing remains dormant, it becomes difficult for any latent, undiscovered thoughts to evolve any further. I would encourage you to return to any 'angry pages' once the heat of the situation has dissipated – you may notice aspects that you had initially overlooked.

Case Study

Michael, a BA Year 2 trainee, was a prolific writer and had immersed himself in the practice of reflective writing with ease. He wrote diligently on an almost daily basis, never returning to the writing but feeling proud to have an archive of his experience of becoming a teacher. During our work together in the first term of Year 2, Michael became intrigued with what he was achieving with his writing, beyond its being a record of events. We decided to look through some of the journal entries together, with Michael identifying pieces that had been particularly significant to him. It soon emerged that his entries fell into two main categories: recaps on sessions or lessons he had observed, and what he described as 'venting' entries that related to issues that had been upsetting or frustrating. By considering the qualities of the writing with me, Michael was able to explore how he could develop his reflections by taking a more analytical approach or by revisiting the more emotive pieces and unpicking them in more depth. Michael found that by loosely categorising his styles of entry, he was able to move beyond descriptive and emotional responses. This heightened awareness nudged him into writing for a wider range of purposes, such as considering an event from another perspective or attempting to analyse an aspect of his practice in a more objective and critical way.

What 'categories' can you identify in your own journal entries?

The role of the other

Let us, then, return to the notion and role of 'the other'. There is a common view that sharing journal writing with a critical friend can enhance the reflective process (Moon, 2006). This 'otherness' is an element of many ITT courses and one that I encourage with my own trainees. The example of Trish's recount allows a glimpse of the pitfalls of writing in isolation. The solitary experience may run the risk of simply reinforcing existing views and perceptions (Boud, 2001, p.14) or leave the writer 'rambling' and going around in circles (Moon, 2006, p.105). I have noticed that among the trainee journal entries I've seen, there is a tendency to ask many questions, questions that often hang unanswered. Sometimes writers tie themselves in knots of unresolved circular thinking and rhetorical questions while struggling to arrive at any form of conclusion (or recognising that there may not always be a conclusion!).

At this point, the opportunity to work in peer groups or pairs may facilitate deeper learning, with perspectives being challenged and support given with areas where writers find themselves stuck. Xie et al (2008) propose that when individuals with different views and values of the world work together, 'it is possible for an overhaul of cognitive structure to take place' (p.20), known as 'transformation' by Mezirow (1991). It can be argued then, that while the capacity of the private writing process needs to be celebrated, so too does the valuable role of the other to help you puzzle through moments of 'stuckness' in your writing.

Once you are in possession of a selection of your own writings, you should be able to identify your own areas of 'stuckness'. Sometimes, when we stare at something for a long time, it becomes very difficult to see it in a different way – this is where the role of the 'other' comes into play. It may well be that in your training, you are encouraged to bring writing into sessions to share with your peers. Group discussion is often of the most benefit here as it offers a range of interpretations. You may feel that you have particular people that you feel comfortable in sharing your writing with, and this is important. However, the process laid out in the activity below should allow you to develop a space where the writing is shared in a collaborative and purposeful way.

Activity
Sharing your writing with others

1. Establish some 'ground rules' with your partner or group. Opening up journal writing to others can feel exposing and, as such, issues such as confidentiality and being sensitive with responses and comments should be agreed on beforehand.
2. Photocopy your journal entry to give to each member of the discussion group. You may want to ask for guidance with a particular issue, or you could just see how the group makes sense of your writing – this can often be very enlightening! Ask them to make notes on your entry, or to highlight any areas that they consider to be significant.
3. You should remain quiet as the group works through your writing. They too should avoid the temptation to discuss the entry with you as they read. While this can feel rather strange, it allows your peers to arrive at their own conclusions and interpretations.
4. Once this process is complete, a discussion can open up about the nature of your journal and particular points of intrigue. You can then reveal more about how the writing was contextualised and respond to any questions that arise. When you gather in the responses, you will have hopefully uncovered different layers to the writing that you may not have been able to see before.

When I have engaged with this activity, I've always been fascinated to see the different ways in which people perceive an event that I had assumed was relatively straightforward!

The realities of being a reflective writer

Stoking the fire

In my role as a tutor, I take a lot of pleasure in working with my trainees and their reflective writing, establishing the right mode of writing for them and encouraging them to seek their own writing sparks. I've found that at the beginning of term, there is usually a real willingness and excitement to get started, but launching the initial act of writing is only the very start of the journey. As the academic year runs along, it is *sustaining* the initial writing that becomes the focus. The dual nature of being a teacher and a trainee throws up many complications and competing demands and you may find that issues such as juggling time or struggling for writing privacy really do interfere with your good intentions. It may be simply that your initial enthusiasm wanes, akin to starting a diary in the New Year and only getting as far as February! It might be helpful to enlist a number of tactics if you suspect your writing isn't flourishing as it should. Perhaps timetabling your writing and finding a solitary space, such as the library, could help. Pre-dating your journal entries might also help you to keep on track. If an extended period of writing isn't available, the use of Post-it notes could help you to capture sparks to revisit at a later point. You may find that simply changing the medium, from paper notebook to blog for example, might re-engage your interest.

Being assessed on your reflective writing

During your teacher training, your reflective journal will undoubtedly fall under the gaze of a tutor or mentor. In some cases, you may be asked to submit your portfolio for assessment. Your school mentor will probably expect to see your reflective writing when you are on placement. My trainees have been quite honest in telling me that this raises a number of tensions for them, in terms of what is expected by tutors and also what they are 'allowed' to write about.

In terms of assessment, your tutor will be looking for shifts in your thinking, and the ability to reflect on your developing practice in a thoughtful and analytical way. The writing should demonstrate that you are moving forward in your practice and beyond the stage of describing things or failing to see issues from a range of perspectives. It is worth making yourself very familiar with the expectations laid out in any assessment criteria you are given.

The dilemma that assessing journals presents is that when writing for assessment, your words may feel subject to scrutiny, and as such, a degree of writing freedom is lost. In the case of school-based writings, it can be very difficult to write honestly about situations that your mentor may not regard in the same way, or even find upsetting. My advice here is to be selective about what you choose to share. It would be very limiting to only write sanitised versions of events that feel suitable for your particular audience. Before you begin, ask yourself – who am I writing this for and how will this impact the way I choose to write it?

Learning Outcomes Review
....

This chapter has highlighted the rewards of adopting the practice of writing reflectively in your journey to becoming a teacher. You should have considered what kind of writing space feels appealing to your own preferred style of learning and how you intend to write in this way. The ideas put forward here are grounded in the reality of lived experiences of busy trainee teachers and it is hoped that by recognising some of the barriers that may present themselves, you will be better armed to sustain your writing and reap the benefits.

Self-assessment questions
1. Write down a list of strategies that you now have to support you with getting started and sustaining your reflective writing.
2. Which of the spaces for reflection do you resonate with the most?
3. Can you identify any barriers that may present themselves in your reflective writing journey? How might you strive to overcome these?

Further Reading

Hatton, N. and Smith, D. (1995) Reflection in teacher education: Towards definition and implementation. *Teaching and Teacher Education*, 11(1): 33–49.
 A useful review of the literature on frameworks and strategies to support the development of reflective writing in trainee teachers.

Lee, H.-J. (2005) Understanding and assessing preservice teachers' reflective thinking. *Teaching and Teacher Education*, 21: 699–715.
A study of the assessment of reflective thinking in trainee teachers and an exploration of how this thinking deepens and develops.

Spalding, E. and A. Wilson (2002) Demystifying reflection: a study of pedagogical strategies that encourage reflective journal writing. *Teachers College Record*, 104(7): 1393–421.
 This study recognises the difficulty that trainees might encounter in writing reflectively and identifies practical ways to engage with and develop reflective writing.

References

Bolton, G. (2010) *Reflective Practice: Writing and Professional Development.* London: Sage.

Boud, D. (2001) Using journal writing to enhance reflective practice. *New Directions for Adult Continuing Education*, 90: 9–17.

Dyment, J. and O'Connell, T. (2010) The quality of reflection in student journals: A review of limiting and enabling factors. *Innovative Higher Education*, 35: 233–44.

Holly, M. L. (1989) *Writing to Grow: Keeping a Personal-Professional Journal.* Portsmouth, NH: Heinemann.

Lee, O. (2010) Facilitating preservice teachers' reflection through interactive online journal writing. *The Physical Educator,* 63(3).

Mezirow, J. (1991) *Transformative Dimensions of Adult Learning.* San Francisco: Jossey-Bass.

Moon, J. A. (2006) *Learning Journals: A Handbook for Reflective Practice and Professional Development.* London: Routledge.

Moore, A. and Ash, A. (2002) Reflective practice in beginning teachers: helps, hindrances and the role of the critical other. Paper presented at the Annual Conference of the British Educational Research Association, Exeter University, 12–14 September.

Schön, D. A. (1987) *Educating the Reflective Practitioner.* San Francisco: Jossey-Bass.

Xie, Y., Fengfeng, K. et al. (2008) The effect of peer feedback for blogging on college students' reflective learning processes. *Internet and Higher Education*, 11: 18–25.

Appendix 1

Model answers to the self-assessment questions

Chapter 1

1. Can you define what reflection looks like for a practitioner and for a child?

Reflection for a practitioner is about learning – identifying good practice and areas that need developing. It can be done formally through a journal, annotating plans, peer feedback and informally through internal dialogue.

Reflection for children is about deepening their learning and enhancing their understanding. Children need a structured framework which guides them and helps the teacher to plan for learning through reflection.

2. What are the different levels of reflection?

- Descriptive Writing
- Descriptive Reflection
- Dialogic Reflection
- Critical Reflection

3. How can you use Bloom's higher order thinking skills to support children's reflection?

Systematically provide opportunities for children to use the higher order thinking skills through reflective techniques:

Understanding – children's reflection is concerned with exploration, thinking and questioning.

Analysis – if you are asking children to 'investigate' as part of their learning objective, then ensure your planning provides appropriate opportunities for investigative learning. Evaluation is more than having an opinion or stating what could be improved. It is concerned with making judgements and defending them with reference to set criteria and/or evidence.

Reflection involves looking at events from different perspectives and this is encouraged through using creative and open thinking.

4. How can you support children's reflective dialogue in the classroom?

- Using 'thinking questions' as part of discussions.
- Planning for reflective techniques in your lessons.
- Providing opportunities for children to talk with themselves and each other.
- Scaffold the use of reflective journals.

5. What is the relationship between reflection and creativity?

Craft (2000) talks of 'possibility thinking' which can be supported through creative ways of learning and further enhanced by reflective techniques. The tools and levels of reflection also aid creative thinking and creative responses through questioning, looking at various perspectives and encouraging internal and external dialogue with others.

6. What difficulties may you face when putting theory into practice and how can these be overcome?

- Time to develop children's reflective skills effectively – plan for this.
- Motivating children to engage with reflection – make sure there is a clear purpose.
- The classroom environment, both physical and social – think carefully about your layout, don't be afraid to move things around and experiment.
- Taking care to use a variety of techniques and carefully considering what you are asking the children to do.

Chapter 2

1. What are the main purposes you use reflection for?

Answers will vary, but you may have thought about purposes such as those listed on page 33. All purposes will lead to an improvement in your professional and academic development.

2. Identify at least one aspect in your current study where you use:
a. informal, intuitive reflection
Informal, intuitive reflection is undertaken during reflection-in-action. It will happen while you are teaching, when you are talking with peers, when you are writing assignments or planning a lesson. This form of reflection happens all the time.

b. non-assessed reflections for another audience
These types of reflections might be of the type in Janet's case study. They might take the form of a reflective journal or portfolio, or an online discussion. Alternatively you may reflect in a letter to a friend or family member as you are writing to them.

c. reflection in assessed pieces of academic work
All your assessed pieces of work will require you to reflect on theory and practice and bring the two together to demonstrate your learning and knowledge about a particular aspect of education. They may not take the form of a structured piece of action research, but may include a part of the action research methodology. The form of the assessed item may also vary, for example it could be a written assignment, a group presentation, or a poster presentation. Evidence of your reflection in practice and on practice and how you can take your learning forward will be required.

3. If you haven't yet done so, visit the first and final activities of this chapter. Use some of the prompts and suggestions in Mike Pezet's coaching chapter to further your action planning.
Answers will vary.

Chapter 3

1. As you consider your lesson planning and weekly planning, how is scaffolding of learning evident within them?

You may identify aspects of the planning process such as resources put in place, adults used and the outcomes you expect. You may also consider the structure of the plan itself and how you have taken learners through the experience step by step.

2. How would you develop your skills more effectively if you drew on Gibbs (1988) model for reflection to evaluate your lessons?

The skills you may develop here may make your evaluation more focused and facilitate a stronger consideration on action as a result. It may help you consider your feelings about the lesson more objectively and make evidence-based decisions.

3. What approaches could you use to reflect on your action?

Approaches you could take may be self-video-recording and using the learning as a result of playback to improve your own practice. You may also consider keeping a learning journal.

4. What will you do if you notice your teaching approaches are not proving effective? How will you change things? What will you learn from this experience?

It is very important that you have noticed. Consider using a greater variety of teaching approaches. Consider using more activity-based approaches. You may find that as a result you arrive at some more effective models of teaching and learning as a result.

Chapter 4

1. To what extent is the focus on children's talk supporting your developing reflective practice?

Answers will vary

2. How would your engagement with other ethical and philosophical questions further support developments in your reflective practice?

Answers will vary

Chapter 5

1. In what situations can you see coaching aiding reflective practice?

- Problem solving situations
- Situations requiring skills development
- Situations requiring problem clarification i.e. is the issue the presenting problem or a deeper underlying problem
- Implementation of learning

- Reflection and learning from experience
- Leadership development
- Relationship development

2. Identify three questioning skills.

- Knowing when open or closed questions are appropriate
- Summarising
- Reflecting
- Non-judgemental questions that stimulate/challenge thinking
- Reframing
- Curiosity
- Interest
- Silence

3. Who 'owns' and is responsible for the outcomes of a coaching session?

The coachee owns the outcomes of the session, the coach is responsible for helping them to clarify their actions and their commitment to those actions before the session ends.

4. What undermines the effectiveness of any coaching, reflective practice session?

- Questions that appear judgemental or push the coachee to feel they need to justify their actions
- Failure to co-design the relationship from the outset, thereby lack of ownership or trust
- Lack of clarity about roles, purpose or process
- Breaking confidentiality without prior discussion
- Lack of listening at level three
- Lack of transparency, for example the coach appearing to push an agenda without being open about doing so

5. Rate your listening skills on a scale of 1 to 10, 10 being very good. Where are you currently? What is working? What would one step up the scale look like? What would you be doing differently?

Answers will vary

Chapter 6

1. Why and how would you plan for self/peer assessment opportunities in your classroom?

You may, for example, plan to incorporate marking ladders into your practice. Marking Ladders can be useful tools to support peer- self-assessment, helping children to decide how well they have achieved a specific target. A marking ladder, for instance, would list all the features which should be evident in children's writing and aids them in assessing their own (see the campaign for learning website).

2. What strategies could you employ in your classroom to help you to reflect on your practice?

One means of reflecting on your practice could be to engage in reflective writing. Reflective writing has the potential to provide you with a systematic approach to your development as a reflective practitioner, and this could be facilitated through regularly writing in a reflective journal to make explicit your position/thoughts/ideas on a range of issues of personal/ professional significance.

3. What opportunities do you have for collaborative teaching?

Drawing on opportunities to work collaboratively could be managed in a number of ways. Making effective use of additional adult support in the classroom could allow for opportunities for you to engage in collaborative teaching. Adopting a team approach to teaching and learning with, for example, Teaching Assistants may prove highly fruitful. However, not all practitioners may have such opportunities and may find that they work in a largely autonomous capacity in the classroom. However, opportunities for collaboration may be capitalised on through joint planning with a colleague based in another class, or through assessment moderation opportunities.

Chapter 7

1. Identify some of the connections and differences between Lesson Study and other forms of professional learning you have experienced. Can you identify features of Lesson Study which will encourage you to try this approach to professional learning?

This model answer may support your response to this question: *Some of the features of Lesson Study are familiar to me. For example, I've had experience of joint planning, but I've never planned a lesson with the focus being on case pupils, and nor have I ever spent so long talking through with a partner exactly what I'd expect particular children to be doing or learning at each point in a lesson (especially thinking about what these pupils would be doing during the teacher-led section). I've also had plenty of people observing my lessons, and have even once had the chance to do a peer observation, but those have always generated feedback on the lines of 'you did this well but you need to work on that'. Lesson Study seems to have a different focus, not on what I did well, but on how far the planned lesson was effective in supporting learning for particular kids.*

2. Reviewing the seven elements of Lesson Study, identify which of them are processes that would be new to you and/ or the people you work with.

This model answer may support your response to this question: *I've tried getting feedback from the children on what they thought helped their learning or what could help more next time, by using questions in the plenary. But the idea of interviewing pupils (and the luxury of having other adults doing that with or for me) is new.*

I've never shared what I've learned about pedagogy with other people in the way that Lesson Study is suggesting, and I feel nervous about doing that, but if I was partnered with my mentor I'd feel more confident in telling people in a staff meeting, for example, what we've done and what helped the children's learning or changed the way we were teaching.

I like the approach of Lesson Study that gives joint responsibility to all the teachers in the Lesson Study group so it's not so intimidating for any one teacher. And I like the emphasis on the children. These are the things that encourage me to try this out on this placement.

3. How might you use Lesson Study in your current professional learning context within the next few months?

Answers will be dependent on context.

Chapter 8

1. Write down a list of strategies that you now have to support you with getting started and sustaining your reflective writing.

Answers will vary

2. Which of the spaces for reflection do you resonate with the most?

Answers will vary

3. Can you identify any barriers that may present themselves in your reflective writing journey? How might you strive to overcome these?

Answers will vary

Appendix 2

Feedback Action Plan
Part Time Primary Undergraduate Programme

During the Programme you have received feedback in written form on your assignment cover sheets. As you progress into each year it is important that you continue to engage with all the feedback that you receive, so that you can continue to improve and develop your skills – and so that you learn more.

One way of making the most of the feedback that you receive is to develop an action plan for yourself. By developing an action plan you make sure that you reflect upon the guidance you have been given and you decide what your next steps are. We would like you to develop the action plan below by undertaking the following steps:

- Review all the assignments you have previously completed.
- Reflect upon all the feedback you were given and complete the following table

Year 1 assignment marks –	Year 2 assignment marks –
Year 3 assignment marks –	Year 4 assignment marks –

Most significant feedback comments:	
Things I did which attracted positive comments:	
Things I can do to build on the positive feedback:	
Things I did which attracted critical feedback:	
Things I can do to address the critical feedback:	

The single most important thing for me to keep doing in my future work on the basis of this feedback:
The single most important thing for me to improve in my future work on the basis of this feedback:

Appendix 3

School Placement – Target Setting and Action Plan

During this academic year you will undertake your Synoptic Placement. This will allow you to develop strong professional relationships with the children and staff. You will also get to know your children very well during this time and be able to cater for their different learning needs during your placement.

It is vitally important to recognise your success to this point. By now you have successfully undertaken assessed placements in two schools and you will have built up a wealth of teaching skills and subject knowledge. The aim of this document is to encourage you to reflect and identify this success while also identifying areas in which you can further develop.

Things I did which attracted positive comments while on placement:	
Things I can do to build on the positive feedback:	
Things mentors/Link Tutors identified as areas for development within school:	
What I have done/can do to address these areas for development?	
Initial School Placement Grade:	
Developmental School Placement Grade:	
I want to complete my next Placement with a Grade . . .	
The one most important thing I need to do to achieve this would be . . .	

Index